BALLOT

Rasheed Kidwai is a journalist, author, columnist and a political analyst. He is a visiting Fellow with the Observer Research Foundation (ORF). Formerly associate editor of the *Telegraph*, Kidwai tracks government, politics, community affairs and Hindi cinema. He is the author of *Sonia: A Biography*; *24 Akbar Road: A Short History of the People behind the Fall and Rise of the Congress*; *Ballot: Ten Episodes that have Shaped India's Democracy*; *Neta Abhineta: Bollywood Star Power in Indian Politics*; *Bharat ke Pradhanmantri: Desh, Dasha, Disha* and *The House of Scindias: A Saga of Power, Politics and Intrigue*.

A graduate from St. Stephen's College, New Delhi, Kidwai holds a master's degree in mass communications from Leicester University, United Kingdom. He also contributes as a political analyst to numerous television channels, including News 18, ABP News, NDTV, India Ahead News and India Today TV.

Praise for the Book

'Kidwai's style is breezy, anecdotal and full of interesting bon mots.' – *The Hindu*

'A fascinating kaleidoscope of India's democratic experience and experiment over the past seven decades... A must-read for all those who are interested in discerning how this chaotic, anarchic land of a million mutinies is also a democratic continuum ever since its liberation from British imperialism.' – *Asian Age*

‘Very interesting vignettes… For both the initiated and the uninitiated, the apolitical and the overly political, the book has something.’ – *Deccan Herald*

‘Kidwai’s book touches upon all major issues in Indian politics that have existed in varying degrees since the early years of Independence – corruption, crony capitalism, welfare schemes, populism, dynasty, gender discrimination, Hindu Right, personality cult, factionalism within the Congress, government–party relationships and land acquisition policy.’ – *Book Review India*

‘Rasheed Kidwai has strung together the small and big episodes, the personalities that shaped our democracy, starting from Indira Gandhi. In this readable, concise account of India’s elected and the elections, all bases are covered…’ – *Week*

BALLOT

TEN EPISODES THAT HAVE SHAPED INDIA'S DEMOCRACY

RASHEED KIDWAI

hachette
INDIA

First published in 2018 by Hachette India
(Registered name: Hachette Book Publishing India Pvt. Ltd)
An Hachette UK company
www.hachetteindia.com

This edition published in 2022

SRD

ISBN 978-93-5195-226-8

Hachette Book Publishing India Pvt. Ltd
4th/5th Floors, Corporate Centre,
Plot No. 94, Sector 44, Gurugram 122003, India

Typeset in Sabon 11/15.7
by InoSoft Systems, Noida

Printed and bound in India
by Manipal Technologies Limited, Manipal

MIX
Paper from responsible sources
FSC™ C043100

Rahmani Bhai and Kauser Apa,
for being the heart of our family

CONTENTS

BALLOT

THE PEOPLE'S MANDATE, BY YEAR

1951–52	1st Lok Sabha, INC Jawaharlal Nehru, 5 years
1957	2nd Lok Sabha, INC Jawaharlal Nehru, 5 years
1962	3rd Lok Sabha, INC 1962: Jawaharlal Nehru, 2 years 1964: Gulzarilal Nanda, 13 days 1964: Lal Bahadur Shastri, 1 year 216 days 1966: Gulzarilal Nanda, 13 days 1966: Indira Gandhi, 1 year 39 days
1967	4th Lok Sabha, INC Indira Gandhi, 4 years
1971	5th Lok Sabha, INC Indira Gandhi, 6 years
1977	6th Lok Sabha, Janata Party 1977: Morarji Desai, 2 years 126 days 1979, Janata Party (Secular): Charan Singh, 170 days
1980	7th Lok Sabha, INC (I) Indira Gandhi, 4 years 291 days
1984	8th Lok Sabha, INC Rajiv Gandhi, 5 years 32 days

1989	9th Lok Sabha, Janata Dal 1989: Vishwanath Pratap Singh, 343 days 1990, Samajwadi Janata Party (with INC): Chandra Shekhar, 223 days
1991	10th Lok Sabha, INC (I) Pamulaparti Venkata Narasimha Rao, 4 years 330 days
1996	11th Lok Sabha, BJP 1996: Atal Bihari Vajpayee, 16 days 1996, Janata Dal: Haradanahalli Doddegowda Deve Gowda, 324 days 1997, Janata Dal: Inder Kumar Gujral, 332 days
1998	12th Lok Sabha, BJP (NDA) Atal Bihari Vajpayee, 13 months
1999	13th Lok Sabha, BJP (NDA) Atal Bihari Vajpayee, 5 years
2004	14th Lok Sabha, INC (UPA) Manmohan Singh, 5 years
2009	15th Lok Sabha, INC (UPA) Manmohan Singh, 5 years
2014	16th Lok Sabha, BJP (NDA) Narendra Modi, 5 years
2019	17th Lok Sabha, Narendra Modi, incumbent

INTRODUCTION

Writing a short book on India's electoral process and indeed the elections as they have played out over the last seven decades is a veritable challenge. The statistics around Indian elections are in themselves mind-boggling. Add to that the drama and drive of parties and personalities, the clash of ideology and agenda, the twists and turns of campaigns and results – this, not just at the national level but across state assemblies and panchayats. I have attempted here to provide an umbrella view of the complexities of the country's political landscape through a selection of what I believe are significant episodes that have decided the trajectory of India's democracy. But before moving to individual analyses it is, perhaps, necessary to go back to the very beginning and set out the landscape in which the roots of India's democracy were planted.

After India won independence from the British Raj on 15 August 1947, the Jawaharlal Nehru-led government had to prepare electoral rolls, formulate and codify election laws, and decide on election processes.

This was no easy task. The Indian National Congress (INC), which had been instrumental in the country's fight for freedom, had made it clear way back in 1928 that universal adult franchise was what would ultimately be adopted as the means for citizens of a free India to choose their representatives in government. House-to-house surveys across the length and breadth of the country had to be conducted to register every single voter. One hundred and seventy-three million voters, both men and women, mostly poor and illiterate, exercising universal adult franchise was a unique experiment in the world.

In a multi-religious, caste-ridden society marked by illiteracy and backwardness in large swathes there was no dearth of those sceptical about the electorate's ability to respond in a politically mature manner. The Western media described India's first general election as 'a leap in the dark', 'fantastic' and 'an act of faith'.

There were two main arguments levelled against universal adult suffrage by its detractors. The first was the magnitude of the task involved. It was argued that the number of voters under adult suffrage would exceed all reasonable bounds and the entire exercise would be too stupendous an administrative task for the new government to handle. The second argument was the illiteracy of most voters. There were fears that the 70 per cent illiteracy level prevailing in the country at the time would render an election a farce unless an electoral system could be devised by means of which every voter could cast a vote secretly and intelligently.

The Constituent Assembly of India, which prepared the Constitution of India, had intensely debated the issue and yet, with full knowledge of the difficulties that would be involved, unhesitatingly adopted the principle of universal adult suffrage. According to Sukumar Sen, India's first chief election commissioner, who supervised the first general election for the Lok Sabha and the 18 state assemblies, granting votes to one and all was an 'act of faith' – faith in the practical common sense of the common man of India. Sen called the decision to adopt universal adult franchise 'a great and fateful experiment unique in the world in its stupendousness and complexities'.

One of the numerous challenges that the nascent election authority faced was that of involving women in the mammoth polling exercise. When electoral rolls were being prepared, Sen and his team discovered that a large number of women voters had not been enrolled under their own names but by the description of their relationship with their male relations (for example, A's mother, B's wife or C's daughter). This, it turns out, was due to local customs prevalent in many north and central Indian states which stopped women from disclosing their names to an outsider. Sen quickly sent instructions to enumerators across the country to insist upon including the proper name of a voter in the electoral rolls. Directions were also issued to the effect that any woman who refused to give her proper name should not be registered, and if she had already been registered without her name, her entry should be deleted. While this was a necessary course of action, the unfortunate effect of the diktat was that out of a total of approximately 80 million women voters in the country, nearly 2.8 million eventually failed to disclose their proper names and missed the chance to cast their vote. Women from Bihar, Uttar Pradesh, Madhya Pradesh and Rajasthan were the most affected.

By the time the 1951–52 polls were held, the new Constitution was in place. The Constitution had made a provision for an independent Election

Commission implying that the poll body would be free of the influence of the executive, the Parliament and the party in power.

In all, candidates of over 14 national and 53 regional or local parties and a large number of independents contested elections for the 489 seats to the Lok Sabha and the 3,283 seats to the state assemblies. Of these, 98 seats to the former and 669 to the latter were reserved for the Scheduled Castes and the Scheduled Tribes. In all 17,500 candidates contested the first election of democratic India.

Since over 70 per cent of the voters could not read or write, a system of using symbols was created. Symbols were assigned to each major party and to each independent candidate. These symbols were painted on ballot boxes and the candidates were identified by these symbols. The voters were to place their ballot paper in the box assigned to a particular candidate in a secret ballot.

Pirojsha Godrej, then a young man, contributed immensely to the successful implementation of this system by producing over 1.2 million steel ballot boxes, one box for every candidate in a polling station. Godrej's factory in Vikhroli, a suburb of Bombay (now Mumbai), comprising a roofed area of 2,33,000 square feet, had to churn out more than 15,000 ballot boxes per day. A newspaper article from that time quoted a Godrej spokesperson saying that if all the nine-inch-long boxes were put on top of each other, they would reach the height of several Mount Everests piled one on top of another.

The polling process in India has undergone a spectacular change since the first election was held, when there were as many boxes in every polling booth as there were candidates. The system of symbols on ballot boxes was used only for the first and second general elections. The system of marking symbols on ballot papers was introduced from the third general election for the Lok Sabha held in 1962, and one box for all replaced multiple boxes. A voter, after receiving the ballot paper from the presiding officer of the polling booth, was to retire to a corner cordoned off for the purpose of casting votes. There they would find on a table a stamp with an 'x' mark and a stamp pad. After marking the stamp against the name of the candidate of their choice, the voter would put the folded ballot paper in the box.

The first general election saw Prime Minister Jawaharlal Nehru leading the Congress from the front. Showing remarkable energy, Nehru covered nearly 40,000 kilometres and directly addressed 35 million people, a tenth of India's population at the time. That the entire election revolved around Nehru was evident from the slogan the Congress had coined: 'A vote for Congress is a vote for Nehru'. The assassination of Mahatma Gandhi in January 1948 had raised Nehru's status to that of a towering leader within and outside the Congress party. His main challenger, Sardar Vallabhbhai Patel, had died in 1950 while Subhash Chandra Bose's disappearance removed the possibility of a radical rival. This had given Nehru unchallenged and unlimited powers in the nascent parliamentary democracy.

Nehru's daughter, Indira Gandhi, who would later emerge as the country's most powerful prime minister, campaigned alongside him, often addressing public meetings. As the election drew closer, Indira took charge of the Raebareli parliamentary seat, from which her husband, Feroze Gandhi, was contesting as a Congress nominee. While, at one level, Nehru, Feroze and Indira were staunch democrats, the roots of the rule of a dynasty were being sown. Feroze's biographer, Bertil Falk, firmly believes that Nehru's son-in-law would have got the Congress ticket even if he was not married to Indira. Feroze was a freedom fighter and had spent four terms in jail. Within the Congress, he had powerful backers such as K.D. Malviya, Govind Ballabh

Pant, Rafi Ahmed Kidwai and Lal Bahadur Shastri. According to Onkar Nath Bhargava, a friend of Feroze, when Jawaharlal Nehru came to campaign for Feroze in Raebareli during the 1952 polls, Feroze seemed worried by Indira's ill-health and curtly asked how many meetings she was addressing each day. It was not just his concern for Indira that made him an unconventional politician. One night, while campaigning, he stayed at the residence of his opponent from the Communist Party, had breakfast there in the morning and then left for campaigning. However, as suitable a candidate as Feroze may have been, the fact that he was Nehru's son-in-law cannot be brushed aside.

Out of the 489 Lok Sabha seats, the Nehru-led Congress won 364, leaving little room for opposition. The Communist Party of India (CPI) won 16 seats while the Bharatiya Jan Sangh (an earlier avatar of the right-wing Bharatiya Janata Party or the BJP) bagged three.

Although fragmented, the Opposition, too, fought the polls with high spirits. Both the Election Commission and the Nehru government earned praise for creating conditions suitable for the unhindered participation of the Opposition parties in the election, including the Jan Sangh and the CPI. However, despite this inclusion, there was no

Leader of Opposition in the Lok Sabha for the next 17 years due to the rules formulated by the first Speaker of the Lok Sabha, G.V. Mavalankar, which stated that a party had to win at least 10 per cent of the strength of the house in order for its leader to be designated as the leader of Opposition.

Although held over six decades ago, many aspects of that first election have contemporary resonance. One of Prime Minister Jawaharlal Nehru's opponents for the Phulpur Lok Sabha seat was Swami Prabhu Dutt Brahmachari, who fought the election on the plank of cow protection. Brahmachari was supported by the Akhil Bharatiya Ram Rajya Parishad and the All India Hindu Mahasabha, two radical right-wing groups. Though he had taken a vow of silence, his pamphlet denounced Nehru as being guilty of allowing cow slaughter in independent India. In the election, Brahmachari garnered only 56,718 votes as compared to the 2,33,571 votes Nehru received, and he lost his security deposit.

In some ways, Phulpur, considered a Congress stronghold, has shown the fluctuating fortunes of the Congress and the efficacy of Nehruvian socialist and secular ideology over the years. Situated barely 35 kilometres from Nehru's place of birth, Allahabad, Phulpur has held pride of place in the annals of the Congress Party's electoral history. Nehru continued to win at Phulpur till his death in 1964. But when, five decades later, the 2014 general election saw the Congress suffering its worst-ever electoral defeat, in Phulpur, for the first time since 1952, a Rashtriya Swayamsevak Sangh (RSS) full-timer, Keshav Prasad Maurya, won with ease.

At a public meeting held at Delhi's Ram Lila Maidan on Gandhi Jayanti in 1951, just a little while before the first general election, Nehru had pronounced the bottom line of the party's secular creed, saying, 'If any man raises his hand against another in the name of religion, I shall fight him till the last breath of my life, whether from within the government or outside.' It is these words that have defined secularism in India for the past seven decades. Secularism, or the separation of religion from politics, has been an integral part of the Congress's ideology. In the Indian context, the Congress's definition of secularism meant equal respect for all faiths and the protection of all religious minorities. The concept of equal respect for all religions had been highlighted in Nehru's report of 1928, and by Mahatma Gandhi at the Second Round Table Conference in London in

1931, where he showcased the party as India's most national and secular organization. Successive Congress resolutions, too, proclaimed that the Congress would translate into reality the guarantees given in the Constitution of India.

Yet, when in 2014, the issue of cow slaughter staged a noisy comeback, Opposition parties in the Parliament, including the Congress, reacted with caution. The BJP, continuing the political legacy of the Jan Sangh, the Hindu Mahasabha and the Ram Rajya Parishad, had won a handsome mandate in the sixteenth Lok Sabha election. Soon after, violent and reckless groups of *gau rakshak*s or cow vigilante outfits emerged and, in the name of protecting cattle, targeted Muslims and Dalits. What was worse was that in many instances the police and district administration remained mute witnesses to an orgy of violence and, on occasion, tried to shield those who were clearly on the wrong side of the law.

The Congress party's mild reaction to the unfolding events and other significant issues such as religious conversion, which are in themselves an attack on the principles of democracy that its founders held close to their hearts, points to a significant shift from its ideological position under Nehru.

Since the first election, Indian democracy has seen more than its share of ups and downs. Yet, if one thing is clear, it is that no political party is above the people's mandate.

1

FROM *GUNGI GUDIYA* TO *GARIBI HATAO*

ON 7 NOVEMBER 1966, THOUSANDS OF *GAU RAKSHAKS*, sadhus and other religious leaders among them, marched down Parliament Street in New Delhi demanding a law banning cow slaughter across the country.

Led by the Bharatiya Jan Sangh member of Parliament (MP) from Karnal, Swami Rameshwaranand, this huge crowd marched menacingly towards the Parliament House complex, clearly meaning to storm it. There was little security to protect the Parliament at the time and the guards on duty hurriedly closed the gates. Infuriated, the agitators went berserk, and began to attack government buildings on Parliament Street.

The police had to open fire, killing seven sadhus. There was widespread condemnation of the police firing and the government's inept handling of the situation. Prime Minister Indira Gandhi, sensing the disquiet, sacked veteran politician Gulzarilal Nanda, who was then India's home minister. Nanda had served twice as a caretaker prime minister when Jawaharlal Nehru and Lal Bahadur Shastri died within a span of less than two years, and was a respected senior figure. He was, however, also a patron of the Bharat Sadhu Samaj and widely seen as sympathetic to the protesters' cause.

This was Indira Gandhi's first year in office and she was fighting on several fronts. Following India's war against China in 1962, Nehru had, according to Marie Seton, an 'air of sad, sorrowing desolation' about him. The issue of his successor was in the air, and contrary to present-day perception, Indira was not the obvious choice. In fact, in 1963 she had been toying with the idea of leaving the country and living in England where her sons Rajiv and Sanjay were studying. In a letter written to her friend Dorothy Norman just 19 days before Nehru's death she said that she 'had to settle down outside India for at least a year and was looking for ways of earning foreign currency to do so'.

Nehru himself had not been grooming Indira as a successor, supporting her rejection of parliamentary seat offers and making no plans for her future. When Indira became the Congress president in

February 1959, Nehru's detractors dubbed it to be the prime minister's bid to push his daughter into the coveted post. However, a large section of the Congress's leaders felt that Indira had earned her post through merit. She was the fourth woman to head the party and quickly proved her mettle by tackling the Kerala crisis, where the E.M.S. Namboodiripad-led government's sweeping land reforms and educational bill that would control the private schools in the state had upset powerful sections of society enough for them to demand his removal, and recommending the creation of Maharashtra and Gujarat to end the linguistic troubles there.

When Indira's one-year term came to an end in February 1960, the Congress Working Committee (CWC) tried to persuade her to stand for re-election, but Indira firmly declined, paving the way for K. Kamaraj to be elected president. Subsequently, she avoided assuming any formal political role but continued to protect her father from people she thought were fair-weather friends. She was also careful to not let her political and social work affect her bond with her children.

Destiny, however, willed otherwise. On 6 January 1964, Nehru suffered a paralytic attack in Bhubaneswar while attending the 68th session of the All India Congress Committee (AICC). In his absence, the prime minister's work was divided between two senior ministers Lal Bahadur Shastri and T.T. Krishnamachari.

Nehru died on 27 May 1964. Nehru's old companion and occasional adversary C. Rajagopalachari gave an apt assessment of Nehru soon after the prime minister's death, saying, 'Eleven years younger than me, eleven times more important, eleven hundred times more beloved by the nation...I have been fighting Sri Nehru all these ten years over what I consider faults in public policies. But I knew all along that he alone could get them corrected.'

Within hours of Nehru's death, the Congress's old guard, informally known as the 'syndicate', closed ranks to elect Shastri as Nehru's successor. K. Kamaraj, a politician among politicians, preferred Shastri over the hardliner Morarji Desai.

According to Pupul Jayakar, a close friend and advisor of Indira, Shastri, before taking the oath of office and secrecy, called on Indira, offering her the prime ministership. 'Indira Gandhi refused,' Jayakar wrote, because 'she felt if she had become prime minister at that time, she would have been destroyed'. Shastri subsequently offered her a ministerial assignment, insisting that without Indira's presence he would not have a stable government. Indira relented and took up the information and broadcasting portfolio.

In September 1965, Pakistan launched Operation Grand Slam in the Chamb sector of Akhnoor in Jammu and Kashmir. Indian troops quickly crossed into West Pakistan at three points, aiming for Lahore. The United Nations brokered a ceasefire agreement on 22 September, with both sides holding some of the other's territory at the end of the war.

Soviet Prime Minister Alexei Kosygin invited both Shastri and the Pakistani President General Ayub Khan to Tashkent in Uzbekistan to work out a settlement. The night Shastri and Ayub signed the treaty, Shastri suffered a massive heart attack and died.

Kamaraj moved swiftly and started projecting Indira as Shastri's successor. A number of senior Congressmen, led by the veteran Morarji Desai, were unwilling but Kamaraj saw a quality in Indira that, according to him, others did not have, 'and he felt that she would win the election in 1967'. Kamaraj, considered a crafty politician, seemed to have felt that Indira's lack of experience and acceptability within the Congress would make her compliant and dependent on him. P.V. Narasimha

Rao would later say that Indira was supposed to be merely a 'vote-catching device' who, after the 1967 polls, would be forced to take a back seat and an experienced person selected to lead the country.

Decidedly against Indira being chosen as the successor, Desai forced a leadership contest within the Congress Parliamentary Party (CPP). Nine days after Shastri passed away, a vote was held among the Congress's elected members and at 3 p.m. the presiding officer handed over the result to Kamaraj in the central hall of the Parliament. Kamaraj announced the winner in chaste Tamil. Few members of Parliament or AICC office-bearers could understand what the Congress chief had said but the suspense did not last long as someone excitedly declared that Indira had won 355 votes to Desai's 169.

Indira swiftly rose in stature and many of the Congress's old guard who had thought of manipulating her were in for a shock. Kamaraj, who had played a great role in shaping her career, was also disappointed when he realized that Indira had a mind of her own and an independent style of functioning. At one juncture, Kamaraj was heard describing her, rather ruefully, as 'a big man's daughter, a little man's mistake', referring to himself as a little man.

Indira was sworn in as the prime minister on 24 January 1966 facing a sandstone statue of the Buddha at the Rashtrapati Bhawan that read 'Be Without Fear'.

Indira may have been fearless, but there were many problems awaiting her attention from the day she took office. The cow-slaughter issue forced her to set up a panel under retired Supreme Court Chief Justice A.K. Sarkar to see if a nation-wide ban on cow slaughter was feasible. She daringly made the then RSS chief M.S. Golwalkar a member of the panel, along with the Shankaracharya of Puri, Dr V. Kurien of the National Dairy Development Board, economist Ashok Mitra and others. Kurien later wrote that Golwalkar admitted to him in so many words that the RSS had launched the November 1966 campaign to embarrass the government and with definite political objectives in mind. The committee's initial mandate was to submit a report in six months' time but it continued to delay the submission until it was dismissed in 1979 by the Moraji Desai's government.

In 1967, the year Indira turned 50, she decided to contest a direct election for the first time, choosing her late husband's constituency Raebareli. Remarkably, she clocked over 25,000 kilometres in 45 days of campaigning. True to Kamaraj's assessment, her personal charisma was phenomenal, but while her popularity ratings were high, the country was struggling on many fronts. The famine and drought that had hit parts of the country in 1966 were so severe that it had led to food riots. Mizo tribals were revolting, and a linguistic agitation was taking shape in Punjab. To make matters worse, a series of scurrilous posters surfaced in Delhi and other parts of the country, emphasizing Indira's alleged 'inauspicious star', reminding people that the day she took oath as prime minister, an earthquake had struck and an Air India plane carrying the scientist Dr Homi Bhabha had crashed, not to mention that she was a widow and, therefore 'tainted'. This was decades before internet-savvy social-media trolls made their appearance but the content being spewed was similar.

The socialist movement was gaining ground in India with 'backward castes' such as the Yadavs, Jats, Reddys, Patels and Marathas becoming disillusioned with the Congress. Ram Manohar Lohia, a former Congressman, felt that the elections of 1952, 1957 and 1962 which the Congress had won with ease, had made voters believe that the Congress could not be defeated. To counter this, Lohia urged a fragmented opposition to field a single candidate against each Congress nominee.

The 'Lohia formula' proved to be a success in the general election of 1967, making a huge dent in the Congress seat tally and leading to the formation of non-Congress governments in nine states.

The Socialist Party would manifest itself as a key opposition in its different avatars. The Bharatiya Jan Sangh also had leaders who were deeply influenced by Lohia's ideology. Lohia and the socialists felt that both Nehru and Indira were not seriously committed to socialism and that while they talked a great deal about socialism they did little in practice to empower the working classes. Big public-sector institutions merely created another set of bureaucrats and industrialists who had no grounding in the socialist ethos.

Indira had chosen Raebareli, the seat her husband Feroze Gandhi had won in 1952 and 1957, and where she had campaigned extensively on his behalf. Located between Allahabad and Lucknow, Raebareli is close to Nehru's Phulpur parliamentary seat. It was first offered to her during the first general election, but Indira had declined it at that time on the grounds that she was raising two young children. During the 1951–52 election, Indira had divided her time between Phulpur and Raebareli, with Nehru commending the fine work she did in a letter he wrote to Edwina Mountbatten in

January 1952. Conscious of the perception of her gender as being 'weak' and seeking to counter it, on 20 January 1967 at Raebareli, Indira invoked her womanhood as a source of strength, earning the informal title of 'Mother India' with a speech where she called the entirety of the country her family and highlighted how she would take care of their burdens. At a public meeting in Jaipur, around the same time, Indira hit out at former royals and took on Maharani Gayatri Devi, who had won in the 1962 Lok Sabha polls by a mammoth margin, getting 1,92,909 votes out of the 2,46,516 cast. Gayatri Devi, a glamorous queen, had fancied herself Indira's rival and worked hard to bring the Swatantra Party, which believed in free enterprise and closer ties with the West, close to the right-wing party Jan Sangh. Launching a direct attack, she asked the voters 'to go ask the maharajas and maharanis how much they had done for the people in their states when they ruled them and what they did to fight the British while they lived in luxury at the cost of the people.'

The March 1967 general election was, however, a blow for Indira. The Congress managed to retain the Centre, winning 283 out of the 520 seats, but it lost nine states. The politically influential Uttar Pradesh slipped out of their hands within a month when Chaudhary Charan Singh left the Congress with a large chunk of MLAs to become the chief minister of a non-Congress coalition.

According to author and history professor V. Krishna Ananth, the 1967 election witnessed an unfolding of the fractures in the nation's social and political edifice with 'the unfolding taking many forms and shapes in the discourse'. What emerged in 1967 was the fragmented socio-political reality of India as a nation which had been stitched together in 1947. The 'experiments in alliances, coalitions and vote appeal on the lines of caste, region, etc.' had a far-reaching impact and continue to influence politics till date.

Indira preferred to answer these developments with silence and surprise countermoves. She split the Congress party to get rid of the old guard. She announced some far-reaching populist measures such as the abolition of privy purses and with a single stroke of her pen, she nationalized 14 leading banks. The last move won the nation's heart and mind. The 'Shoe-shine Boys Union' offered to shine for free the shoes of all AICC delegates as a show of their gratitude towards the party.

The biggest bank to be nationalized was Central Bank, controlled by the Tatas with deposits of over ₹4 billion, and the smallest was the Bank of

Maharashtra with deposits totalling ₹700 million. Indira had struck a severe blow to other big business houses too such as the Birlas who were running United Commercial Bank, the Dalmia–Jains who ran Bharat Bank and its 292 branch offices, the Punjab National Bank that had been set up by Dyal Singh Majithia, Lala Harkishan Lal, Lala Lajpat Rai and others, along with some Gujarati entrepreneurs who had big stakes in Dena Bank. An economic survey of 20 leading banks of that era showed that 188 people who served as directors were also directors of 1,452 companies. The large funds that they had used to acquire private profit and privileges were now open for public good – to finance the rural sector of the economy, lend money to farmers to purchase tractors, allow taxi-drivers to purchase cabs and so on.

Indira Gandhi returned to power in the early polls of 1971, with the powerful slogan '*garibi hatao*'. Emerging as a towering, powerful prime minister, Indira's greatest moment of glory came when Pakistan was split into two. The surrender of thousands of Pakistani troops in Dhaka and the creation of Bangladesh capped her triumph, earning her the title of 'Durga', the demon-slaying goddess, from none other than Atal Bihari Vajpayee of the Bharatiya Jan Sangh.

2

FROM ARTICLE 352 TO 153 SEATS

INDIA'S DECISIVE VICTORY IN THE 1971 WAR AGAINST Pakistan restored national pride, which had been damaged after the 1962 skirmish with China. President V.V. Giri took the lead to confer the Bharat Ratna, the country's most prestigious civilian award, on Indira Gandhi.

In an article titled '*Kiski Puja Kar Rahe Hain Bahujan*' ('Whom are the lower castes worshipping?'), published in 2001, Prem Kumar Mani, a Dalit activist and politician, recalled that Jan Sangh leader Atal Bihari Vajpayee had called Indira Gandhi an 'Abhinav Chandi Durga' for defeating Pakistan. The article also mentioned that communist leader S.A. Dange protested against this strongly, saying 'Atal Bihari does not know what he is saying and Indira Gandhi cannot understand what she is hearing. Both should know that Chandi Durga massacred Dalits and backward classes.'

Modesty, or Dange's remark, may have prevented Indira from accepting Vajpayee's compliment with the words 'I am only Indira and I want to remain so,' but she admitted to her friend and biographer Pupul Jayakar that she had had some intimations of 'supernatural powers throughout the war and even previous to it, having had strange experiences'. Jayakar thought that Indira was filled with euphoria and this left little space for any other emotion or doubt. The Pokhran nuclear tests in 1974, which made India the world's sixth nuclear power, further enhanced Indira's stature both in the country and abroad. The annexation of Sikkim in 1975 turned her into a towering personality who could do no wrong.

A personality cult emerged around her. Conscious of her bitter experience with the Congress's old guard, she tried to take total control of the Congress as an organization. Many powerful chief ministers were shunted out and replaced by her favourites, for instance Barkatullah Khan who replaced Mohanlal Sukhadia in Rajasthan, and P.C. Sethi who took the place of S.C. Shukla in Madhya Pradesh. Indira also made deliberate attempts to control the party funds that were crucial for elections as well as all other political activities, making the party and the government dependent upon her for survival.

There was another factor that contributed immensely to the changes occurring in the Congress's functioning as an organization and as a party. In 1969, Indira's younger son Sanjay returned from England after having been trained at the Rolls Royce factory at Crewe. Sanjay, then 23 years old, applied for a license to manufacture a small and cheap car in India. When he turned out to be the lone applicant to have been granted a license, charges of nepotism started doing the rounds. The matter was raised in the Parliament and the house saw Indira pursing her lips and shrugging off the criticism. But there was more to follow. The Congress government in Haryana led by Bansi Lal handed over 300 acres of land for Sanjay's car factory, for which some 15,000 peasants were evicted. P.N. Haksar, who was the principal secretary to Indira till 1973, was fired for opposing Sanjay's project.

On the other side of the political spectrum, this period saw the emergence of Jai Prakash Narayan, a freedom fighter who had been living quietly in Bihar. JP, as he was popularly called, was a young man in 1921 when Nehru and Maulana Abul Kalam Azad had spotted him. He had spent considerable time in various British jails. However, his ties with

Nehru turned sour soon after independence and he joined the rival Socialist Party.

In 1973, JP wrote to several MPs seeking to protect individual rights and democratic values. He formed a body called 'Citizens for Democracy' and became a sort of patriarch for disgruntled elements. His followers multiplied day by day. Sanjay became a favourite target of his at a time when some publications hostile to Indira and the Congress were publishing exaggerated stories about Indira's son turning into a monster.

Sanjay's rise also coincided with the rise of a small but powerful clique within the Congress that often functioned parallel to the prime minister's office and had Sanjay at the helm. At Indira's residence, a special telephone line was installed in Sanjay's room, from where Indira's additional private secretary R.K. Dhawan remained constantly in touch with chief ministers of the Congress-ruled states, the police commissioner and Lieutenant Governor of Delhi along with several influential party and government functionaries. The modus operandi was to make calls and issue instructions for and on behalf of the prime minister's son while, on many occasions, Indira was not even aware of Sanjay's growing unconstitutional clout.

On 12 June 1975, the Allahabad High Court

declared Indira's 1971 parliamentary election in Raebareli null and void because of electoral malpractice. More importantly, it debarred her from holding any public office for the next six years. While Indira struggled to face the situation, her close advisor Siddhartha Shankar Ray came up with a proposal to invoke Article 352 of the Indian Constitution and proclaim an internal emergency. On 25 June 1975, a public rally was organized at Delhi's Ram Lila Maidaan where Morarji Desai, JP and other leaders asked Indira to step down. The next morning, Indira proclaimed a national emergency citing 'threats to national security'. Chaos ensued, with Opposition leaders being arrested, a clamp down on the freedom of the press and, a little while later, a ban proposed on grass-roots organizations such as the RSS and its affiliates.

The declaration of emergency was not unusual in developing countries like India. Even in Britain, the Edward Heath government had called for a national emergency five times during its rule. In India, too, an 'external' emergency had been declared during the 1962 and 1971 wars. But in the summer of 1975, there was nothing to justify it. Political scientists and scholars of that era felt that if individual states like Bihar were facing problems, a presidential decree would have sufficed. In 1978, the Shah Commission, which was set up to examine the Emergency and its excesses, found that there was no evidence of a threat to the Constitution or law and order that had warranted the Emergency.

Sanjay Gandhi's activities during the Emergency were questionable and occasionally bizarre. Indira, however, had a different take on them. After the defeat of 1977, noted film-maker Khawaja Ahmad Abbas sought an appointment with the former prime minister. Abbas gave specific instances of Sanjay's excesses, ranging from forced sterilization of people to inciting violence, but Indira made no attempts to defend him or herself. Instead, she praised Sanjay's simplicity and sincerity, blaming her party chief ministers, the CWC and other AICC office-bearers for 'building up a false image of Sanjay'. She claimed to have written numerous letters to chief ministers of Congress-ruled states asking them not to accord state receptions but said they had insisted on lionizing Sanjay.

Significantly, during the Emergency, a constitutional amendment was introduced. The 42nd Amendment, enacted in November 1976, after the Lok Sabha's five-year term had expired, purported to reduce the power of the Supreme Court and the high courts. It also declared India to be a socialist, secular republic and laid down the duties of Indian citizens to their government. One of the main authors of this amendment was D.K. Barooah, who, as Congress president, had immortalized himself by coining the slogan 'India is Indira, Indira is India'. When the bill was brought up in the Parliament, A.R. Antulay, a barrister from Lincoln's Inn, too, praised Indira and called for a 'fresh look at existing constitutional provisions like five-yearly parliamentary polls'. As if there was a battle for excellence in flattery, Bansi Lal outdid both Barooah and Antulay when he told Indira's cousin B.K. Nehru to change the provisions and 'just make her the President of India for life'.

By January 1977, Indira realized that the Emergency would have to be ended. She called for fresh election, dissolved the already stretched Lok Sabha, released political prisoners and braced for polls. The Emergency, with all its limitations, had not done irreparable damage. Individual and political freedom still existed within it and political opponents were not shot. Even the most draconian provisions of the 42nd Amendment had not abolished the Supreme Court and had not ended the electoral process.

The decision to declare the end of the Emergency was also perhaps due to the fact that the era failed to usher in any significant social or economic reforms to compensate for the absence of democracy. That the Congress party could not be rid of its democratic ethos was evident from the manner in which the Congress MPs themselves voted to repeal much of the 42nd and other Emergency-era constitutional amendments when the Janata Party came to power.

In a nutshell, Indira and Sanjay's flirtation with dictatorship taught most Indians about the dangers to democracy. It educated them about demagoguery, about the perils of hero-worship, and about disregarding liberty and placing power in the hands of a few. It taught them that, like the fight against McCarthyism in the United States, vigilance was the constant price that citizens would have to pay to ensure that an event like the Emergency was never repeated.

The Congress party's electoral defeat of 1977 was huge. Both Indira and Sanjay lost in their respective constituencies. In Uttar Pradesh, which had 84 Lok Sabha seats, the party drew a blank. There were similar stories all over north India. Indira had perhaps sensed it coming. While campaigning in Raebareli, she asked London-based industrialist Swaraj Paul to check with BBC's Mark Tully how she was doing. Tully bluntly presented a grim picture. At the dinner table, Indira turned to Paul to check the BBC correspondent's assessment. Paul reproduced in a low voice what Tully had said in a much harsher tone. To Paul's surprise, Indira was far from upset and remarked that Tully 'was correct in his assessment'.

The Congress ended up with 153 seats in the Lok Sabha against the Janata Party's 298 seats. The Janata Party, comprising the Congress (O), the Bharatiya Jan Sangh, the Sanyukta Socialist Party and the Bharatiya Lok Dal, had hurriedly come into existence barely a month before the general election and was a mix of socialist and right-wing ideologies. The Jan Sangh, backed by the RSS, was an influential player and when the Janata Party government was formed, it had Atal Bihari Vajpayee and L.K. Advani as senior ministers.

The RSS viewed the Emergency as the 'second freedom struggle'. Many years later, the BJP-led Shivraj Singh Chouhan government in Madhya Pradesh announced hefty monthly pensions (ranging from ₹8,000 to ₹25,000) to the thousands of political activists who were detained under the Maintenance of Internal Security Act (MISA) and the Defence of India Rules (DIR) during the Emergency.

Much of the RSS's literature even claims that it was the RSS and the Jan Sangh that had saved democracy in India during the time. The role of peoples' movements has been underplayed in RSS journals and books and a subtle attempt has been made to project the Sangh Parivar as the people who opposed the Emergency. Arvind Rajagopal, a scholar and author of *Hindu Nationalism and Reshaping of Public in India* thinks that the Emergency provided the Jan Sangh and the RSS with an element of respectability which subsequently paved the way for its later avatar, the BJP, to enter mainstream Indian politics. The importance of the Emergency in the growth of the RSS and its later-day political face, the BJP, needs to be emphasized, according to Rajagopal, because it helped them place Hindutva in a wider historical process rather than in fanaticism.

Interestingly, the abrupt fall of the Janata regime also had a lot to do with the RSS. When Chaudhary Charan Singh and other members revolted against Morarji Desai, the socialist lobby raised the issue of 'dual membership', objecting to the Jan Sangh's presence in the Desai government. The Janata Party had a code for its members that determined that they could not join any other organization whose objectives were at variance with it, and Jan Sangh members in the Janata Party were linked to the RSS.

By the time Indira returned to power in 1980 by exploiting the Janata Party's inherent contradictions, ideological divides, and one-upmanship, her zeal to promote secularism and socialism, watchwords throughout the early 1970s, seemed to be missing. She sought to cultivate the majority community, even accepting an invitation to launch the Vishwa Hindu Parishad's (VHP's) 'Ekatmata Yatra'. This was a nascent VHP's first mass-contact programme, providing a sign that Hindu rituals and symbols could be effectively utilized for popular and political mobilization. A clear indication came from her loyalist C.M. Stephen who declared in 1983 that 'the wave-length of Hindu culture and the Congress culture was the same'. Barely six months before her assassination, she sought to assure the majority community that 'the integrity of the country would be in peril if any injustice was done to them'.

Rajagopal feels that in the absence of any comprehensive history of the Emergency, the RSS successfully manufactured an account of democratic struggle that it claimed existed mainly due to the Sangh. Gandhi's assassination had made the RSS a political pariah but after the Emergency, acquiring political power was within their grasp.

The Congress's first-ever defeat since the Independence saw an exodus of its members from the party. But the fighter in Indira was far from disturbed. Some senior party leaders, including the then Congress president Brahmananda Reddy, announced on the first day of 1978 that Indira had been expelled from the party. The split cost Indira dearly. Indira headed a Congress faction called Congress (I) while Brahmananda Reddy's faction was called Congress (R). Apart from losing the support of 76 out the 153 members of the Lok Sabha, her new party also became homeless and she lost the party symbol of the cow and the calf.

Indira was reportedly relieved to let go of the cow and the calf, as it had been ridiculed throughout the country – the cow was seen as Indira and the calf as Sanjay. Indira asked for the old party symbol of a pair of bullocks, but the Election Commission had frozen the symbol by then. Buta Singh, who, as the AICC general secretary at that time, had a room at 24, Akbar Road, petitioned the Election Commission for a new symbol. Indira was out in Vijayawada with Narasimha Rao when Singh was asked by the Election Commission to pick a symbol and the choices given were an elephant, a bicycle and an open palm.

Unsure of which symbol to pick, Singh booked a call to seek Indira's approval. The line was probably not clear or, perhaps, Singh's accent was thick but

Indira kept hearing *haathi*, or elephant, instead of *haath*, or hand, when it came to the third option. She kept refusing even as he tried to explain that it was not the elephant but the open palm symbol that he was advising her to pick. An exasperated Indira handed the telephone to Rao. In a matter of seconds, Rao, a master of more than a dozen languages, understood what Singh was trying to convey and reportedly shouted out to Singh to call it a *panja*. Relieved, Indira took the receiver and wholeheartedly agreed.

Although discarded by Indira then, the cycle and the elephant are alive and kicking even after all these years – in Uttar Pradesh, as the symbols of the Samajwadi Party and Mayawati's Bahujan Samaj Party, respectively.

3

THE BIG TREE AND THE SAPLING

THE 1977 AND 1984–85 GENERAL ELECTIONS ESTABLISHED beyond any doubt that the RSS was capable of taking tactical positions for the advancement of its larger political goals. In 1977, it directed the Jan Sangh to merge with an entity like the Janata Party that had a sizable presence of socialists and breakaway Congress factions. The idea behind the merger was to further the Sangh's interests, both short- and medium-term.

When the eighth Lok Sabha election was announced in 1984, after the assassination of Indira Gandhi and the brutal anti-Sikh riots that had followed in retaliation, the country was passing through perhaps its biggest political turmoil since the Partition and Mahatma Gandhi's assassination. The RSS supported a Congress that was led by a young man with little experience in politics or governance.

Their move was significant on several counts. Their new political entity, the BJP, had been formed in 1980 and it was facing a major test during the 1984–85 polls. Kuppahalli Sitaramiah Sudarshan, later to become the *sarsanghchalak* (head) of the RSS, held that all political parties were equal in the eyes of the RSS as long as they served the broad RSS agenda of cultural nationalism, *swadeshi* and Hindu renaissance. Their support for the Congress days after Indira Gandhi's assassination was evident in an article authored by veteran RSS ideologue Nanaji Deshmukh published in the Hindi magazine *Pratipaksh*, which he ended with a call to bless and cooperate with Rajiv Gandhi when voting was less than a month away.

Indira had been assassinated for the drastic actions she had taken to curb separatism in Punjab. In post-Independence India, Sikhs felt they had not gotten a fair deal during the 1947 Partition of the country. This feeling was accentuated when several linguistic states were created but Punjab was denied the right of a Punjabi-speaking state. The demand for a Punjabi *suba* (province) was conceded in March 1966 by splitting the original Punjab into Haryana, Himachal Pradesh and Punjab when Indira had just taken over as prime minister.

Indira had had serious reservations about creating

a Punjabi-speaking state. She felt that conceding to the Akali Dal's demand was a reversal of a long-held Congress position. Even after the creation of a Punjabi *suba*, the Akali Dal launched an agitation seeking Chandigarh for their state, and upped the ante by passing the Anandpur Sahib resolution that sought to recast the constitutional structure and toyed with the idea of an elusive Sikh homeland.

Indira and Sanjay, in order to tame the Akalis, had Union Home Minister Giani Zail Singh bring in Sant Jarnail Singh Bhindranwale, an obscure Sikh priest, into politics. Bhindranwale, a fiery zealot, helped the Congress during the 1980 Lok Sabha polls but then brought about a wave of violence – killing his political opponents almost at will, stroking communal passions against Hindus, and raising a trained battalion of militants and terrorists – until the Akali leadership caved in and joined hands with him.

By early 1984, many senior police officers, leaders of civil rights groups, religious leaders and media personalities in Punjab had been killed, paralyzing the state's government and forcing Hindus to flee. At this time, Indira received disturbing reports about the Golden Temple at Amritsar, the high seat of the Sikh clergy, being turned into a fortress and housing a large number of militants trained in guerrilla warfare by a retired and decorated general, Shahbeg Singh.

On 2 June 1984, the prime minister broadcast an appeal to the Akalis to not stop the movement of food grains from Punjab to the rest of the country. The very next day, the army moved in, laying siege to the Golden Temple in an operation codenamed 'Blue Star'. The timing of the army's storming of the temple was unfortunate as it was the day of the martyrdom of Guru Arjun Dev and the shrine was packed with devotees. The army had to neutralize rocket launchers even as its battle tank Vijayanta moved in, trundling down the marble steps right up to the holy tank. Heavy 105 mm guns were used to flush out the terrorists reportedly hiding in the rooms around the tank. The majestic Akal Takht, the spiritual seat of the timeless, built by the Sixth Guru Hargobind in the early 17th century, was reduced almost to a rubble.

Outrage and a sense of disbelief prevailed across the nation, even leading to sporadic incidents of mutiny in the otherwise extremely disciplined Indian army. S.S. Gill, who was the secretary, Information and Broadcasting, recalled seeing Sikhs, their hair dishevelled and shock writ large on their faces clutching chunks of the demolished Akal Takht.

Giani Zail Singh, a Sikh and a staunch Indira

loyalist, was the President of India when the Akal Takht was demolished. He defied government advice and visited the Golden Temple on 8 June and 'wept like a child'. But his sense of outrage had no impact on the Sikh clergy which excommunicated him.

Blood-curdling threats were made against Indira and her family. The prime minister was specifically asked to remove Sikh guards from her personal security, but she refused saying, 'Are not we secular?'

As if she had a premonition of what was to come, on the fateful morning of 31 October 1984, Indira, it is said, did not want to let go of Priyanka, her granddaughter, as she left for school. She hugged the girl tightly and reminded her grandson Rahul to not cry in the event of her death. Sonia, her daughter-in-law, had just finished washing her hair when she heard what she thought were crackers bursting nearby. Then she heard the maid crying and rushed outside shouting, 'Mummy, oh my God, Mummy'. There was utter confusion and when the car carrying the world's most powerful woman reached All India Institute of Medical Sciences (AIIMS) there was nobody there to receive her. At 2.20 p.m., Indira Gandhi was officially declared dead.

Indira's older son, Rajiv was in West Bengal and heard the news en route as he flew back to Delhi. As soon as Rajiv reached Delhi, P.C. Alexander, principal secretary to Indira, and other trusted aides, told him that the Cabinet and the Congress party wanted him to be the prime minister. Alexander said he had to make a determined bid to tear Rajiv away from Sonia at AIIMS. Sonia pleaded with Rajiv not to consent, but Rajiv believed that it was his duty to do so.

The young prime minister quickly announced a general election, to be held ahead of schedule between 24 and 27 December 1984. Rajiv's election campaign was aggressive and focused on making the Sikhs seeking a separate homeland a key issue. The hidden agenda was to somehow exploit insecurity within the Hindu community and project the Rajiv-led Congress as their sole saviour.

The election saw an immense wave in Rajiv's favour with the party winning 415 out of the 543 Lok Sabha seats, a tally that his mother and illustrious grandfather had both failed to achieve. He had travelled over 50,000 kilometres by car, helicopter, and aeroplane in 25 days of campaigning. There were talks of a secret meeting between Rajiv Gandhi and the then RSS chief Balasaheb Deoras resulting in the RSS cadre supporting the Congress in the 1984 Lok Sabha election despite the presence of the BJP in the political scene. The BJP, however, has denied any understanding between the RSS and the Congress under Rajiv Gandhi.

India Today showered lavish praise on the new leader of the Congress party, exclaiming that 'the results had demolished the myth of a political novice'; *Time* magazine dubbed the results a 'mandate for change, for cleaning up and for efficiency'; and *Newsweek* likened Rajiv to John F. Kennedy. For the first, and perhaps the only time, 24, Akbar Road, the AICC headquarters in New Delhi was illuminated for three days in celebration of the party's grand victory.

The general election of 1984 had a massive impact on domestic politics. The newly formed BJP was decimated – winning merely two out of the 543 parliamentary seats. Rajiv Gandhi had lined up Amitabh Bachchan and Madhavrao Scindia to compete for seats against veteran politicians Hemvati Nandan Bahugana and Atal Bihari Vajpayee, and the latter had both been humbled.

Rajiv's rise had a massive impact on the Congress party too. Many veteran leaders who had been close to Indira and Sanjay found themselves left out in the cold. Rajiv's *durbar* was a mix of technocrats, politicians, mavericks, and time-servers. While there were advisors like P.V. Narasimha Rao, and N.D. Tiwari, and professionals like P. Chidambaram and Mani Shankar Aiyar, there were also masters of political manipulation like Buta Singh and Sitaram Kesri.

One of the bigger names to lose out in the Rajiv era was Pranab Mukherjee, an Indira loyalist who used to be number two in her cabinet. Years later, Mukherjee would criticize Rajiv Gandhi's excessive reliance on a few close friends and advisers, calling them 'mere fortune-seekers'. On being dropped from Rajiv's cabinet, Mukherjee pointed out that the age difference between him and Rajiv was only nine years but 'their temperaments and backgrounds were vastly different'.

On 31 December 1984, a new cabinet was sworn in. Before the swearing-in, newly elected Congress MPs met in the Parliament. According to those present there, Mukherjee, standing next to Rajiv, had a fixed smile on his face. Next to him were three debutant members – Amitabh Bachchan, Vyjayanthimala Bali and Sunil Dutt.

Rajiv Gandhi had a scandal-free image when he came to power, but his image as 'Mr Clean' did not last long as major scandals like the Bofors scandal, the Fairfax scandal and the HDW submarine-deal scandal soon exploded. Owing to his political naivety, Rajiv failed to showcase many of his achievements such as the priority he accorded to technology, education, and infrastructure development as well as the economic reforms he initiated. S.S. Gill later observed that the tragedy of Rajiv Gandhi was not that he failed to fulfil his promises but that he ended up aligning with the same forces that he had vowed to fight against.

By the time Rajiv was voted out of power in 1989, the moral and administrative fabric of India had been corrupted to the core. The decline had begun during Indira's tenure and the Emergency, but by 1989 respect for law, human dignity and the rights of an individual were no longer talking points in the country's administrative culture.

4

FROM THE WILY FOX TO ONE MORE PUSH

ON 20 MAY 1991, RAJIV AND SONIA GANDHI ARRIVED AT New Delhi's Nirman Bhawan to cast their votes at around 7.30 a.m. Just behind them stood Rajesh Khanna, once a Bollywood megastar and now the Congress nominee for the prestigious New Delhi constituency. They were the first to vote and the polling booth bustled with enthusiastic Youth Congress and Sewa Dal – the party's training wing – volunteers. Snap polls had been announced after the dramatic ouster of the Chandra Shekhar government that had held office between November 1990 and June 1991. Chandra Shekhar was a former Congressman and a bitter critic of the 'Nehru–Gandhi dynasty' but had ironically been propped up by the Congress party's 197 MPs in Parliament. The Congress withdrew support from his government on the flimsy ground that his government was spying on Rajiv Gandhi. The real reason, it seemed, was Rajiv's political assessment that he was poised to return as India's prime minister.

Soon after returning from voting that morning, Rajiv left to resume the back-breaking election campaign that had seen him travel several thousand kilometres in the past weeks. He was putting all he had into the campaign to try and make up for the Congress's defeat of 1989. Sonia kept pleading with him to take a break but he was unrelenting.

Twenty months in the Opposition benches had made Rajiv much wiser. He deeply regretted the way he had frittered away the massive mandate of 1984. The Congress's strength in Parliament had plummeted from 404 in 1984 to 197 Lok Sabha seats in 1989. However, by 1991, things were looking up as the public mood was turning against shaky coalitions and their power games.

In his zeal to win at all costs, Rajiv was defying an intelligence bureau advisory to not hold public meetings after sunset in Tamil Nadu, where Sri Lankan Tamil separatists, who posed a significant threat to his life, had huge pockets of support. Such advisories, for Rajiv, however, came in the way of interacting with the crowds at his rallies and he largely ignored them.

The next day, on 21 May, Rajiv boarded a helicopter for a whirlwind tour of the coastal areas of Bhadrak, Angul, Gunupur and Paralakhemundi in Orissa before crossing over to Vishakhapatnam in Andhra Pradesh. Uma Gajapati Raju was the Congress nominee there. Rajiv was a great votary of getting young professionals into politics, and he had made a special effort to get her a ticket.

According to Suman Dubey, Rajiv's press adviser, who accompanied him on the campaign, the former prime minister was unusually late that day, but once he was up and about, he took off addressing a series of meetings in Orissa and Andhra Pradesh before moving out to Tamil Nadu. Rajiv reached Madras at 8.30 p.m., met the press for 10 minutes, had a soft drink and then hurriedly left by road for Porur to address a public meeting. At 9.30 p.m. he held another meeting before heading for Poonamallee. In between these engagements, Rajiv gave interviews to Neena Gopal of *Gulf News* and Barbara Crossette of the *New York Times*. Gopal claimed that Rajiv had commented on how South-Asian leaders were cut down just as they were about to achieve something, and within minutes of making that bone-chilling prophetic statement, Rajiv Gandhi himself was gone. She was catapulted from an unknown reporter to someone who would always be known as the last journalist to have interviewed Rajiv Gandhi, minutes before he died. She went on to call it 'a macabre twist and not the kind of exclusive I had bargained for'.

At Sriperumbudur, there was little by way of security arrangements. Constables from the Tamil Nadu police watched curiously as Rajiv mingled freely with the crowd. Rajiv's personal security attendant, Pradeep Gupta, made a feeble bid to keep the mob from touching him. Senior state Congress leaders, ranging from G.K. Moopanar to Margetham Chandrashekhar, were sitting on the dais about a 100 yards away. Rajiv began walking briskly while accepting garlands from everybody. He stopped when he heard a poem being recited by Kokila, young girl. It was at this time that his assassin, Dhanu, moved closer to him carrying a garland made of sandalwood. An edgy Rajiv must have sensed something unusual and signalled to the constable near him to regulate the crowd. But by then Dhanu had bent, pretending to touch Rajiv's feet, and detonated the RDX strapped to her. Ironically, at the time of the blast, a chorus at the public meeting was still singing, 'Rajiv Gandhi's life is our life; if not for Indira Gandhi's son, there is no life for anyone'.

Although Rajiv was not occupying any official

position when he was assassinated, more than forty dignitaries – royalty and heads of state among them – from around the world attended his funeral and offered their condolences. The funeral itself took place near Shakti Sthal, Indira's *samadhi*, and was attended by a vast crowd.

Rajiv's assassination was followed by a brief period of confusion. There was no clear mechanism for succession in the Congress. Indira and Rajiv Gandhi's hold had dismantled the post of number two in the party. Well past midnight after Rajiv's assassination, senior Congress leader Arjun Singh was outside 10 Janpath looking on as a small group of party workers, reportedly loyal to him, chanted, 'Sonia *lao*, *desh bachao*'.

Singh proposed Sonia's name for Congress president and other Congress leaders endorsed it. The deliberations took place while Rajiv's body was still lying in state. The CWC's decision was communicated to Sonia by a group of party leaders consisting of Ghulam Nabi Azad, Pranab Mukherjee and others. Sonia did not say anything, but she must have been taken aback by the timing of the request. A day later, she issued a small statement refusing to accept the post. Friends of the family said that Sonia and her children did not even consider the offer.

When the jockeying for Rajiv's successor began,

Sharad Pawar and his followers were quick to take the lead. Pawar was counting on the support of almost all the party MPs from Maharashtra, while his arch-rival Arjun Singh had no such luxury. Singh decided to reach the pinnacle of Congress politics via 10 Janpath. He became a die-hard Sonia loyalist in the hope that one day 'Madam' would recognize his devotion, loyalty and worth.

Many congressmen wanted the then Vice President of India Dr Shankar Dayal Sharma to step down from his post and take charge of the party. Sharma, a scholar of repute, a freedom fighter and a Nehru–Gandhi loyalist, who had also been a Congress president, also wanted to become the prime minister. The moment Sonia turned down the CWC's plea to succeed Rajiv, his followers swung into action. Sharma almost made it, too, despite Arjun Singh's opposition – he lost the battle at the last moment when Narasimha Rao edged him out.

Rao was so low-key that the others never really considered him to be in the fray at all. But it was on him that the mantle fell. Rao's formal election as leader of the Congress was not very dramatic as the six other contenders had virtually given up. Once the Congress MPs were convinced that Sonia wanted Narasimha Rao to be prime minister, a mock election was arranged. The venue was 24 Akbar Road. Rao polled more than 95 per cent of the votes. Barring a handful of die-hard Pawar supporters, everyone voted for him.

When Rao took over as prime minister in 1991, at the age of 71, little was known about him. While he had many friends and admirers in Delhi, his long stint there had made him an outsider in his native state of Andhra Pradesh.

For Sonia, though, Rao was a bit of an unknown entity even if it would seem he had been chosen by her. She respected him as a senior leader of the party. Indira had been extremely fond of him, giving him key assignments in spite of the stiff opposition from many towering leaders from Andhra Pradesh such as M. Channa Reddy, Brahmanand Reddy and Vijay Bhaskar Reddy. In fact, Rao was one of the few to have access to her residence. Rajiv, too, had found much to admire in him, including his low-key style of functioning and his ability to defuse even the most volatile situations.

Both Sonia and Rao were reticent individuals, and after he took over as prime minister, the two hardly spoke to each other, preferring to deal with each other through Wajahat Habibullah and Ramu Damodaran. Habibullah, an IAS officer of the 1967 batch from the Jammu and Kashmir cadre, was drafted as the chief executive of the Rajiv Gandhi Foundation (RGF) that was headed by Sonia, while Damodaran was private secretary to Rao.

Within days of taking over as prime minister, Rao made a gesture that deeply touched Sonia. He had been appointed as a trustee of the RGF and there was a tussle as to where the first RGF meeting should take place. Sonia was keen to have it at 10 Janpath, but some people close to Rao raised the issue of protocol. Habibullah and Damodaran saved the situation when the latter communicated Sonia's request to Rao, pointing out that she was in no mental condition to visit 7 Race Course Road since it used to be Rajiv's office. Sensitive to her feelings, Rao called up Sonia and told her that he would be coming over to 10, Janpath. However, the outside world misconstrued Rao's kind gesture as a sign of the country's prime minister paying obeisance to a private citizen.

It has been said that Rao's inept handling of the Ayodhya dispute, his focus on economic reforms, the tardy probe into the Rajiv Gandhi assassination case and allegations of corruption contributed to creating a deep wedge between 10 Janpath and 7 Race Course Road. In retrospect, these do appear to be contributing factors, but the real reason was Sonia's belief that Rao was systematically trying to undermine the Nehru–Gandhi legacy.

In the general election of 1991, the Congress emerged as the largest party with 244 seats, largely due to a sympathy wave caused by Rajiv Gandhi's assassination. When Rao took over as prime minister, the Indian economy was in bad shape. Due to fiscal imbalances, foreign reserves were down to just two weeks' requirements for imports. Drastic measures were required. Both the International Monetary Fund and the World Bank were keeping a hawkish eye on the situation. Given that Rao was leading a minority government – Rao had formed the government with the support of smaller parties and the communists – his government's capacity to take hard decisions was in question.

Rao picked economist Dr Manmohan Singh as his finance minister. (Singh would later serve as the prime minister for 10 long years between 2004 and 2014.) Senior Congress leader Jairam Ramesh described the period between 21 June and 24 July 1991 as not only an intellectual revolution, but also an evolutionary one with both the crisis and the response some years in the making.

While Rao did exceedingly well to bring the economy back on the rails, his handling of the

Ayodhya dispute left much to be desired. In his book, *Ayodhya 6 December 1992*, Rao made the singular point that 'the BJP aborted any solution to the Ayodhya dispute to keep the Ayodhya pot boiling'. Till August 1992, Rao says, his talks with 'apolitical' sadhus and sanyasis on how and where a Ram temple could be built in Ayodhya lawfully and peacefully were proceeding quite well. Then, all of a sudden, the sadhus broke off talks. Four months later, the Babri Mosque was demolished by hordes of *kar sevak*s. Rao was of the opinion that the political forces behind the demolition scuppered the talks to keep a vote-rich communal issue alive.

Rao's five-year tenure was a curious mix of achievements and failures. With the help of Dr Manmohan Singh, who was then finance minister, Rao stabilized the economy, introduced flagship schemes such as mid-day meals for all school-going children and infrastructure projects but faced serious allegations of corruption. He failed to be a popular leader within the Congress and the party's defeat in the 1996 general election did not seem to come as a surprise to Sonia Gandhi.

It was in the third week of December in 1997 that Sonia Gandhi first indicated her willingness to take a more active role in politics. It was

Priyanka and Rahul who assisted Sonia in making up her mind to join active politics. The family was collectively convinced that it had to fight the BJP as they believed the party was bent upon destroying all the good that had been achieved from the time of Nehru's leadership through to Rajiv Gandhi's. Contrary to popular belief, it was Rahul who influenced her more than Priyanka. He offered to quit his job in London to help her, a gesture that deeply moved Sonia. On 28 December 1997, the 112th anniversary of the Indian National Congress, Sonia chose to go public about her intention to join politics.

After the general election was announced, on 11 January 1998, Sriperumbudur became the venue of her first public meeting. The outcome of the election to the twelfth Lok Sabha, however, came as a shock to the Congress. After a gruelling campaign that saw Sonia address 130-odd meetings cover over 40,000 kilometres, the Congress's final tally read 142 seats. Atal Bihari Vajpayee of the BJP became prime minister, heading a rainbow coalition of regional parties. Vajpayee would go on to rule for six years as he won another round of general election in 1999, becoming the first non-Congress prime minister to complete a full term in office.

5

FROM THE LOTUS TO THE *HAATH*

IN THE MOST DRAMATIC GENERAL ELECTION SINCE INDIRA Gandhi was driven out of power in 1977, another Gandhi led the nation's oldest party back to power after eight years on the Opposition benches.

Sonia Gandhi's favourite phrase is said to be, 'They do not know the stuff I am made of'. Pitted against heavy odds, Sonia proved herself emphatically on 14 May 2004 by leading the Congress to an unexpected victory. She was the Congress's lone campaigner, addressing 90 public meetings in one fortnight and travelling over 70,000 kilometres. Although she drew crowds, her opponents constantly poked fun at her, even calling her a 'Jersey cow'. But her grit kept her going.

Sonia's role as campaigner has to be put in context. She had no support whatsoever from other notable leaders in the party. Going by the number of appearances, apart from Sonia, Priyanka and Rahul, the most popular campaigners from the Congress were Govinda, Sunil Dutt and Dilip Kumar. Almost the entire CWC remained confined to Delhi. Manmohan Singh travelled little. Given the good doctor's seniority and grip over economic issues, Congress managers had arranged for his interaction with prominent citizens and chambers of commerce. One such meeting scheduled for him in Indore was called off as Singh did not feel 'up to it' and had problems explaining complex economic issues in Hindi. He had never been either a mass leader or a vote catcher. In spite of his hard work for the 1999 general election he had lost the election from south Delhi by 30,000 votes and the defeat had made him somewhat reclusive.

Other Congress stalwarts included Kamal Nath, who remained in Chhindwara from where he was contesting, Digvijay Singh, who fought and lost in Rajgarh, and Arjun Singh, who toured reluctantly to a few places but failed to win even a single seat.

In spite of these hurdles, the Congress emerged as the single largest party in Parliament and came in 30 seats ahead of its competition, the BJP alliance – a conclusion that no exit or opinion poll had predicted. 'Victory and defeat are a part of life, which are to be viewed with equanimity,' said the outgoing Prime Minister Atal Bihari Vajpayee in an address to the nation, capping a day of searing shocks to his party and the National Democratic Alliance (NDA) he had led for six years.

The Indian voter left the NDA – and possibly also the Congress alliance – blinking in amazement as their mandate for 2004 unfolded. It will never be known if the voters had surprised even themselves. Pollsters, internal assessors, astrologers – they were all proved wrong.

Leading newspapers across the globe carried the results on their front page. The Italian newspaper *Corriere della Sera*'s headline ran, 'Italian Sonia Gandhi triumphs'. The *Guardian* called the result a complete surprise to everyone but the people who matter in an Indian election. The *Times* commented that the country had always surprised the world, especially when its unpredictable 660 million voters decided the country's future, further opining that the defeat of the NDA government, led by Atal Bihari Vajpayee, must rank as one of the greatest election upsets of all time, matched only by the defeat of Churchill in 1945 and Truman's victory in 1948.

The general prognosis had been that the NDA would 'somehow' make it and that the Congress was destined to be in the Opposition for another five years. The general election of 1999 had been held in September of that year, but the 2004 general election were advanced by six months by the otherwise sagacious and wise Vajpayee. Pramod Mahajan, Venkaiah Naidu, Sushma Swaraj and a number of other BJP office-bearers had reportedly convinced Vajpayee to declare the election early, pointing out that they should take advantage of the prime minister's ratings being at an all-time high in January 2004. Given all this, the announcement of the general election of 2004 by the Election Commission on 29 February 2004 could not have come at a worse time for the Congress. The general election was being held barely three months after the party's severe drubbing in the state assembly polls for Madhya Pradesh, Rajasthan and Chhattisgarh. The Congress was ill-prepared on several counts and for the first time since 1998, when Sonia had formally taken over as party chief, Congressmen had begun to doubt her ability to lead the party.

The Vajpayee regime launched the 'India Shining' campaign, a media blitz showcasing improved India–Pakistan relations, a buoyant economy and the mega projects launched by them such as the golden quadrilateral highway to emphasize the point that Vajpayee and the BJP should be given another chance to make India a 'global superpower'. This campaign was the country's most glitzy publicity exercise after the Congress campaign of 1984, when images of India under siege after Indira Gandhi's assassination had worked wonders for the Congress.

The Congress managers realized that there was no way they could match the high-decibel BJP campaign, especially given the party's paltry budget of ₹20 crore. Instead of going out with a mega campaign, the party focused on their regional strategy. In a span of months, from the beginning of March till May, 3,000 insertions appeared in the press. Of these, 80 per cent were in regional media. The Congress also severely lacked other resources. It had fewer aircraft and choppers and mobility and visibility of the candidates was an issue but Sonia worked hard to achieve her goals.

Five major national news networks and scores of newspapers and magazines came up with their opinion and exit polls predicting a Vajpayee–NDA victory. One exit poll gave the Congress as low a tally as 92 to 102 seats. The highest estimate gave it 190 to 205 seats – a prediction that came close to the eventual number of 216.

Interestingly, two days before 14 May 2004, the day the Lok Sabha results were to be declared, Anil Ambani called on Sonia Gandhi. Ambani's presence at 10 Janpath when results were yet to be announced, created a stir. A BJP general secretary was heard saying that the Ambani gut feeling seldom went wrong. When the results were announced on 14 May 2004, it became clear that the BJP had only itself to blame. As part of the run-up to the 2004 polls, the BJP had jettisoned two reliable team mates: the Dravida Munnetra Kazagham (DMK) and its comprising parties, including the Pattali Makkal Katchi (PMK) and the Marumalarchi Dravida Munnetra Kazhagam (MDMK), and the Indian National Lok Dal. The result was a wipeout in Tamil Nadu and only one seat in Haryana.

The Congress, on the other hand, did not allow memories of Rajiv Gandhi's assassination, the LTTE and the DMK 'link' and the Jain Commission report to cloud its political imperatives. It cemented a coalition with the DMK and the Left in Tamil Nadu, a state which had eluded its grasp for decades. The alliance worked wonders and resulted in a complete sweep of the state by the Congress.

The BJP had also made the mistake of rebuffing the Asom Gana Parishad (AGP) in the knowledge that they, the BJP, had emerged as the 'anti-Congress's pole in Assam. The AGP belied this claim by getting a sizeable number of votes that helped the Congress pick up nine Lok Sabha seats from the state.

In Maharashtra, the Congress alliance with the Nationalist Congress Party (NCP) came in handy in offsetting the anti-incumbency sentiment against the Sushil Kumar Shinde government.

The other states where alliances came in handy for the Congress were Bihar – though the Rashtriya Janata Dal (RJD) gave them only four seats – and Jharkhand, where the Congress–RJD–JMM combine swept the polls.

The 2004 general election also heralded the entry of Rahul Gandhi, the fifth generation of the Nehru–Gandhi family since Motilal Nehru, to enter politics. By January 2004, Rahul had begun to take greater interest in the forthcoming election, becoming visible in almost all the strategy meetings. His management background and political instincts gave Sonia a much-needed boost. For instance, it was Rahul who prevailed upon Sonia to go 'all out' on her 'roadshows'. He urged her to reach out to the masses and understand what they want. He was also instrumental in coining the slogan 'Congress *ka haath, aam aadmi ke saath*'.

On 21 March 2004, an auspicious day in many parts of the country on account of the celebration of regional festivals such as Gudi Padwa and Ugadi, Rahul was named the party nominee from Amethi, which used to be Sonia's parliamentary constituency. It was a deft move. Rahul was fielded from Amethi after Congress managers conducted a secret in-house survey. The results of the survey conducted across 134 Lok Sabha constituencies in the country showed that Vajpayee was ahead of Sonia. It was clear that the only way to even out Vajpayee's advantage was to field Priyanka as well as Rahul alongside Sonia. Like his father Rajiv Gandhi, Rahul was made party general and then elevated to vice president of the party under the watchful eyes of Sonia. In the next decade, Rahul has emerged as another power centre in the party.

After the Congress's victory, even as Sonia began to hold talks to form a government and appealed to the Communist Party of India (Marxist) (CPM) and the CPI to join a Congress-led coalition, the RSS said it would be a 'disgrace' to have an 'Italian leader' as prime minister, referring to Sonia Gandhi's foreign origin. Senior BJP leader Sushma Swaraj announced her resignation from the Rajya Sabha and threatened to shave her head if Sonia was made prime minister. K. Govindacharya, a

BJP ideologue, along with Uma Bharti, launched a *rashtriya swabhiman andolan* – or a national self-respect movement – to protest against Sonia being made prime minister.

Sonia, however, remained silent. From the evening of 14 May till 17 May, she told everyone that very shortly a Congress-led coalition would be in place. During this period, she earned an unequivocal endorsement from the Congress's allies to take over as the prime minister of India, setting the stage for her swearing-in that very week if she so wished. This unanimous expression of confidence in Sonia Gandhi came on the same day the Sangh Parivar stepped up the chorus against her foreign origin and threatened to launch a 'national movement' against her.

After four days of suspense and speculation, Sonia finally declined to accept the post of prime minister, saying that her long association with the Nehru–Gandhi family had moulded her to think of the larger interest of the nation and nothing else. She became the first leader of a democratically elected parliamentary party in India to decline the post of prime minister.

Appealing to her beseeching supporters to allow her to make her own decision, she said she was listening to the call of her 'inner voice'. Fighting to make herself heard above indignant shouts from MPs, she pleaded with them to accept her decision and to recognize that she was not going to reverse it.

Informing the President formally about her decision on 19 May 2004, she said, 'The nation is safe in the hands of Dr Manmohan Singh.'

To the outside world, Manmohan Singh was an economist, a theoretician and a man known for his integrity and poise. Within the Congress, he was a popular figure because he had consciously stayed away from factional politics. He had always remained by Sonia's side, yet nobody had ever dubbed him as part of any coterie. On his part, Manmohan Singh did not let Sonia down and the two functioned as a team that enjoyed an instant rapport and understood each other well. Both were reticent, hated media attention and avoided the old political culture of sycophancy and false promises.

Why did Sonia opt out of the race? Was she reluctant from the very first day? Was she unsure of leading a rainbow coalition containing unpredictable allies? Did she consider herself inexperienced? Closer scrutiny shows that none of these factors influenced her while declining the country's most sought-after job. In truth, Sonia responded to being challenged by a section of her countrymen, however small a minority, who were uncomfortable at the prospect of her becoming the prime minister of India. She dreaded the prospect of Congress workers battling in violent clashes with Sangh Parivar activists, and the thought that someday, somebody, driven by xenophobia, would try to set themselves on fire horrified her. She was convinced that the office of prime minister was not worth that.

As news of Sonia opting to not take up the country's top job was being flashed on television, Narendra Modi must have heaved a sigh of relief and smiled. Perhaps nothing would have been more embarrassing for Modi than having to interact with Sonia had she become the prime minister since it was he who had launched a sustained campaign against her foreign origin and ridiculed her aspirations to become the political head of the country. Modi's controversial Gaurav Yatra, which started from Phagvel in Kheda district of Gujarat in September 2002, was essentially directed at the Congress president who was being slammed as 'Italy *ki beti*'. Congress supporters were described as people wearing 'Italian glasses' who could not see reality. Modi's Sonia-bashing continued throughout the state assembly election in December 2002, which the BJP won, and into the general election, where it performed miserably. While the Congress doubled its tally in Gujarat, the BJP lost six seats from its 1999 tally, managing to retain only 14 of the 26 seats.

Writer Sumit Mitra has compared Sonia's act of renunciation to Julius Caesar's abdication. 'Just as Julius Caesar thrice refused the crown that was offered to him by the citizens of Rome, so too aeons later, in Delhi's sizzling summer, did Sonia Maino Gandhi turn down the request of the majority of the Fourteenth Lok Sabha's elected members to accept the prime minister's mantle. If Caesar declined kingship to become the republican leader, Sonia's refusal was perhaps the product of a more complex web of issues.' Mitra felt that while 'at one level, it may have been realpolitik of an exceptionally high order...it is also the imprimatur of a deep ethical conscience.'

To cynics, Sonia's act of renunciation was a clever ploy to keep the prime minister's position warm for Rahul Gandhi, run the Manmohan Singh government remotely and reward loyalty at all levels. But, as with any other sphere, politics is a complex field, too filled with imponderables to be guided by a script. A closer look at future developments confirms this.

6

FROM THE CMP TO MODI *SARKAR*

THE TEN YEARS FOLLOWING THE 2004 ELECTION AND Sonia Gandhi's refusal to become prime minister saw the Congress-led United Progressive Alliance (UPA), headed by Prime Minister Manmohan Singh, struggle with dual power centres. Rahul Gandhi, projected as the heir apparent, kept his focus on inner-party democracy, but failed miserably in turning the grand old party into a modern, progressive, accountable political outfit. Despite Manmohan Singh's sincere and repeated offers to Rahul to join his council of ministers, the latter declined. In December 2009, Singh told the news network CNN–IBN that he had tried many times to induct Rahul into his Cabinet, but had not succeeded so far. Calling him not just an inspirational leader but also a 'fine gentleman', Singh asserted that Rahul's best was yet to come.

Rahul's potential as a leader has been a popular subject of discussion for many years now, both within the party and outside it. Many senior Congress leaders feel that if Rahul had served as a minister of state and later moved on to foreign affairs, or a ministry handling infrastructure, he would have had a markedly different standing in public life. Instead, he bought the *durbari* argument that, as a member of the Nehru–Gandhi family, he should settle for nothing less than prime ministership.

As a fallout of this, the tussle between the government and the party – which had seemingly been settled in favour of the former during the tenures of Jawaharlal Nehru and Indira Gandhi, both powerful prime ministers – was reopened and ultimately led to the downfall of the Congress to the extent that its very survival became uncertain.

Before India's Independence, the Congress was a movement rather than a political outfit, and largely united in its political aims. However, after 1947, once it became the ruling political party, the clash between the head of government and the head of the party escalated. Matters came to a head when the Congress chief at the time, Acharya Kripalani, tried to force Nehru to consult party stalwarts before taking crucial administrative decisions.

On the strength of his pre-eminent status, Nehru snubbed Kripalani's plans to 'guide and advise' the government. Kripalani had failed to realize that the top party leadership had formed the government and only second-tier leaders were left to run the Congress. And that, after all, the tail could not wag the dog.

The tussle continued and intensified as disagreements between Prime Minister Nehru and Deputy Prime Minister Vallabhbhai Patel came to the fore. In 1952, Purushottam Das Tandon, a man known for his soft Hindutva views and a Patel loyalist, was elected to the position of party president, replacing Kripalani. Tandon clashed head-on with Nehru on issues of secularism and their on-going wrangle resulted in Nehru humbling Tandon by getting the members of the CWC to support him in his ideological standing and to hand in their resignations. Tandon was forced to resign from his post and Nehru thereafter took over as the party president, sealing the matter. When Indira Gandhi came to power, she too proved to be a strong prime minister and ensured that the party president played second fiddle to the head of government.

This is the way it stayed in the Congress till, between 2004 and 2014, Sonia Gandhi reversed the equation. As Congress president and its star campaigner, Sonia had far greater power and political legitimacy than her handpicked prime ministerial nominee Dr Manmohan Singh, no matter how competent he was.

While Pranab Mukherjee has claimed in his memoir that he was under the impression that in 2012 he would be made prime minister and Manmohan Singh would be sent to the Rashtrapati Bhawan as the President, sources close to Sonia insist that this had never been considered. It's not too difficult to understand why Singh was preferred over Mukherjee for the post of prime minister a second time running. After Narasimha Rao, 10 Janpath was wary about whom they would appoint. Though Sonia was officially not in politics then and played little role in Rao's appointment as Congress president and prime minister after Rajiv Gandhi's assassination, she was aware of the games Rao and his team had played. Rao was reportedly of the thought that Sonia, lacking in political experience, was becoming a 'puppet' in the hands of some of his arch-rivals within the grand old party. On Sonia's part, she slowly started believing that Rao was out to systematically undermine the Nehru–Gandhi legacy. Her close associates namely V. George, K. Karunakaran, Arjun Singh,

M.L. Fotedar, Natwar Singh and others seemed to have promoted this line of thought. Denying the prime ministership to him was not a reflection on Mukherjee in particular but a reflection of her general distrust towards the political tribe.

When Manmohan Singh was elected as the leader of the CPP, the CPP Constitution was amended to create the post of a chairperson more powerful than the CPP leader. Sonia Gandhi was made chairperson of the UPA, and the head of a National Advisory Council (NAC) set up to act as a driver for policy-making in government. The advisory council was packed with socialist–leftist thinkers and non-government leaders (some with plenty of grass-roots experience) who often had scant regard for the political system. Most NAC members enjoyed the status of cabinet ministers without any accountability. The salary and perks of the 10 NAC members and their 35 staffers were decided by the Prime Minister's Office (PMO). According to a former minister in the PMO, who spoke off-the-record, Singh dreaded visits from members of the NAC. One source recalled that members of the NAC would even, in defiance of protocol, address the prime minister by his first name.

The NAC was credited with pushing the National Rural Employment Guarantee Act (NREGA) later renamed the Mahatma Gandhi National Rural Employment Guarantee Act (MNREGA), the Right to Information Act (RTI), the domestic violence bill, the food security bill, the nutrition policy for children, the tribal resettlement policy, the forest rights act and the communal violence bill, but in passing these bills it continually clashed with the bureaucracy and the political establishment. The Common Minimum Programme (CMP) that was worked out hurriedly in 2004 had turned into a sacred book for the UPA regime. It was packed with populist measures that seemed to have left little room for infrastructure development and economic growth. Many in the ambitious middle class began to view the UPA government as one that did not care for them and members of the NAC were criticized for not knowing how to balance their social aims with the reality of the country's finances. The BJP in particular sharpened its attack on the NAC as it felt the body gave Sonia the status of a 'super PM'.

Sonia's reliance on the NAC highlighted the absence of the Congress party's intellectual capability to influence government policy and bureaucracy. Traditionally, in a parliamentary democracy, party leaders have their ear to the ground while legislators remain sensitive to their constituents' problems. The NAC was neither here nor there. Throughout the ten years of the UPA's rule, 24 Akbar Road, the Congress headquarters in Delhi, contributed little in terms of either generating new ideas or sending any concrete proposal from the party to the government. Some old-timers even wondered if the Congress leadership had assumed a negative role with its functionaries acting to kill or blunt any fresh initiative rather than utilizing the talent available with them.

Meanwhile, in the government, Singh's senior ministers fought bitterly among themselves, even as allegations of high-level corruption relating to the 2G spectrum, coal bloc allocations and the Commonwealth Games were raised by both the far right and those seeking transparency in public life. The various acts of omission and commission in the alleged coal scam were the most glaring.

Similarly, environmental clearances were handled tardily. There was open talk of industrialists being forced to pay a tax of sorts. The minister in charge, Jayanthi Natrajan, became so controversial that Narendra Modi openly talked about a 'Jayanthi tax' – an allegation that went virtually uncontested.

In another instance, a minister of state refused to clear a coal project that the prime minister was personally keen to launch. Repeated attempts were made by the PMO to make the minister see reason, but he did not budge. Often, the minister, now deceased, was heard flaunting his proximity to a senior AICC functionary and claiming that he could not be 'harmed'. This led to Singh's detractors privately describing the prime minister as a 'super-cabinet secretary' who had the freedom to address issues ranging from administrative reforms to the pension bill but not of actually following through.

The environment ministry's functioning during the UPA's second term upset even Congress chief ministers. A particular chief minister shared with this author how a noted industrialist offered to get the state's project cleared. 'I felt small,' the chief minister said on the condition of anonymity, 'that a business house had powers to intervene and get things done in a matter that was between the centre and a state government run by the same political party.'

The progressive RTI measures adopted by the UPA also played their part in harming the government's image. Genuine and not-so-genuine RTI activism almost paralyzed the decision-making process because the system did not have enough safeguards to defend decisions taken in good faith by the bureaucracy. Both Sonia Gandhi and

Singh repeatedly asked for governance to become transparent even as bureaucrats tried to resist 'file notings' (the *written* remarks, observations, recommendations, opinions added by bureaucrats on the files they worked on) from being made public.

The right to work scheme, MNREGA, was spread indiscriminately across India causing labour shortages in a labour-surplus country. A Federation of Indian Chambers of Commerce and Industry (FICCI)-KPMG report titled 'Labour in Indian Agriculture: A Growing Challenge', showed that the MGNREGA affected farm labour adversely and had a negative impact on productivity and prices. The report found that between May 2004 and December 2011, farm labour declined by around 30.57 million while the total size of the workforce kept rising. The share of agriculture in the workforce during the same period declined from 56.7 per cent to 48.8 per cent.

Both Sonia Gandhi and Singh were also great believers in tokenism. Be it the selection of a new President, the home minister, the Speaker, the heads of various boards and commissions and other key appointments, the UPA leadership looked for token empowerment on gender, caste, and community lines. It did not work at all but rather promoted mediocrity at the expense of merit. Ministers like Jairam Ramesh opposed industrialization in the most backward regions of the country under the erroneous and patronizing assumption that *adivasi*s and the inhabitants of those areas did not have material aspirations beyond mere subsistence.

During the UPA years, a core committee consisting of the prime minister and the home, defence and finance ministers used to meet every Friday at 10 Janpath to interact with Sonia and her political secretary Ahmad Patel. But crisis management was always a low priority. One such instance involved the then army chief General V.K. Singh's reported 'defiance' against the government. General V.K. Singh, currently a minister of the Modi government, had courted several controversies while in service, one of which had been giving a newspaper interview saying that he had been offered a bribe for clearing the purchase of Tata trucks and that he had informed the then defence minister about it. This was in 2012 when the UPA regime under Singh was already battling troubles on several fronts, including charges of corruption. To counter General V.K. Singh's statements, the defence ministry prepared a case for his summary dismissal and a draft letter was prepared in consultation with the PMO. But at the core committee meeting, Defence Minister A.K.

Antony developed cold feet and pleaded with Sonia to not sanction General Singh's dismissal. Prime Minister Manmohan Singh reportedly remained silent on the matter and the issue was allowed to die down. When General Singh subsequently joined the BJP, he won the Ghaziabad parliamentary seat in 2014 by a massive margin of votes, second only to Narendra Modi's in Varanasi.

Towards the end of his tenure, Manmohan Singh became aloof from affairs of the state. He maintained the status quo vis-a-vis Pakistan and Jammu and Kashmir. When a brutal gangrape in Delhi in December 2012 outraged the country, Singh made sure that the Lieutenant Governor of Delhi Tejendra Khanna was not harmed by angry mobs. Sonia threw a protective ring around the Delhi Chief Minister Sheila Dikshit who had become thoroughly discredited by this time. By the time the Delhi assembly polls were held, Dikshit lost her own assembly seat to Arvind Kejriwal.

While in office, Manmohan Singh also faced serious and often embarrassing situations. In a parliamentary democracy, the prime minister primarily draws power from his ability to hire and fire members of his council of ministers. Singh lacked that mandate. Firstly, he was confronted with heads of alliance parties like Sharad Pawar, Laloo Prasad

Yadav, Dayamani Maran and Ram Vilas Paswan holding key portfolios. These individuals ensured that the prime minister had no powers to assess their performance, or intervene in key policy matters, or even the senior appointments they made. Worse, there were numerous instances of these individuals functioning in accordance with their whims and fancies. In one instance, a minister sat for over six months on a decision to import wheat, leading to spiralling prices and inflation.

There were some inherent structural problems as well. Congress ministers often functioned rather independently. Ministers went public on issues such as defending or opposing the creation of special economic zones (SEZ), confronting the Reserve Bank of India (RBI) governor on the issue of foreign banks being permitted to open more branches and ATMs, and farm sector reforms. Added to this was the much discussed issue of National Security Adviser (NSA) M.K. Narayanan's close relations with 10 Janpath. Narayanan took over the post of NSA after the untimely death of seasoned bureaucrat J.N. Dixit who had worked hard and independently to strengthen the UPA government's standing in every way, particularly in the areas of foreign policy and internal security. Narayanan's 'cop-like' approach to political and diplomatic initiatives with Pakistan, China and Nepal, as well as domestic issues like Kashmir and the Maoist problem, were perceived as a weakening of the government's stand.

Yet, Singh's contributions too cannot be ignored. Significantly, he introduced a new work culture in the government. While ministers like Arjun Singh, A.R. Antulay and Meira Kumar indulged in rhetoric on sensitive issues, Manmohan went around handpicking lieutenants and associates, all of them experts and seasoned in policy-making, who called the shots on key policy issues. Apart from Montek Singh Ahluwalia, who emerged the third most powerful person in the UPA after the prime minister and Sonia, team Manmohan Singh included highly skilled members of the Planning Commission, heads of the finance commission and the scientific advisory council, and the interlocutors for behind-the-scenes talks with the US, Pakistan and China. Singh also seemed to have sensed the direction of the wind as far as ultra-nationalistic wave went, and is known to have wondered in private conversations why the Congress leadership was not promoting a 'Hindu mainstream face' to check Modi. He was perhaps conscious of his own minority status along with that of Antony, Sonia and Ahmad, all key decision-makers in the government. Of the other senior Congress leaders, both P. Chidambaram and Pranab Mukherjee lacked popular support in their home states and Rahul, despite Singh's insistence, refused to join the government. When a proposal to promote young ministers of state namely Sachin Pilot, Jyotiraditya Scindia, Milind Deora, R.P.N. Singh, Jitin Prasada and others was made, it was shot down by 10 Janpath because they were all second-generation dynasts. The decision again led to a dearth of powerful political players who could draw voters.

Thus, despite Singh's efforts, all was not well with the UPA's standing in the nation and by 2011–2012 the party had to contend with a series of poll debacles, allegations of corruption, the slow pace of economic reforms, the rise of Anna Hazare and the India Against Corruption movement and Sonia Gandhi's mysterious illness. Another big blow came in the form of international credit rating agency Standard & Poor criticizing the UPA government for 'policy paralysis', drift and lack of accountability.

While the UPA was struck by inertia, the rival camp was working on a meticulous strategy to come to power. A section of business magnates, Hindu religious orders, retired bureaucrats, members of intelligence community, gurus as well as media houses began zeroing in on Gujarat Chief Minister Narendra Modi as the prime ministerial candidate from the BJP. A large number of professionals joined as volunteers for mission 2014 giving time, money and ideas to promote the notion of 'progressive change'. The building of 'Brand Modi' was not an organic event but a careful strategic operation carried out in meticulous detail. The '*Abki Baar Modi Sarkar*' campaign was brilliant, and in some ways surpassed former US President Barack Obama's much-touted campaign of 2008.

On 16 May 2014, many records were broken. The BJP, on its own, won a historic 282 seats – a good 100 more than its previous highest tally of 182 under Atal Bihari Vajpayee in 1998 and 1999. It was the first time since 1984 that a party had crossed the halfway mark without forming alliances, which spelt the end of the coalition era though Modi took NDA partners into the government. Modi chose to stay away from Delhi on the day of his victory and entered the national capital a day later with all the pomp and flair of a conquering emperor. With this election, the Congress saw its lowest-ever tally since the 1951–1952 polls – winning only 44 seats. The Modi juggernaut crushed the 128-year-old party, leaving it in tatters in the face of a resurgent, impatient, youthful India.

The 2014 general election was a game-changer in many ways. The Congress's opponent in this election was not the BJP per se, but rather the 'Modi wave' which had been gaining ferocity over the past years. Modi, who had been the Gujarat chief minister since 2002, had cleaned up his Hindutva image and stepped away from the aftermath of the Gujarat riots of 2002. Not only that, he had built up an image of progress, development and transparency that was in direct contrast to what the Congress seemed to have projected of themselves in their decade in power.

But it was not just this image makeover that set Modi apart but also his use of all available mediums to propagate said image. Narendra Modi registered a website under his name in the same year as the Indian National Congress. As a person, he was a brand – and he left no stone unturned in building it up. He was accessible, he was visible, he was present at youth festivals such as Manthan (it later turned out that his team was a large part of the organization to begin with) and he came across as knowing what he was talking about. There was no chatter about the wrongs of the present government, but rather his campaign to become the prime minister was a positive one (unlike in the 2017 Gujarat assembly election). People were willing to listen to him and, more importantly, to trust him. For the first time, a politician this powerful was extremely active on social media. He blazed the screens – his interview with Rajat Sharma in *Aap ki Adaalat* was telecast multiple times and has 16,080,927 views on YouTube. Here was a man, it seemed, whom every one could relate to, who was talking the talk and seemed to have already walked the walk in Gujarat. That Modi came to power was not really surprising. The kicker was that he did it so completely.

After his victory, Modi brought in close associate Amit Shah as BJP national president. A controversial figure who had gone to jail in 2008 for setting up allegedly fake 'encounter' killings and had been barred from visiting Gujarat because of a Supreme Court order, Amit Shah emerged as an astute political player. Shah's association with Modi dated back to 1982 when he was an RSS activist and Modi was a *pracharak* in charge of youth activities in Ahmedabad's Maninagar. When Modi became chief minister in 2001, he tapped Shah's talent as a political player and subsequently handed Shah crucial portfolios, including home, parliamentary affairs, law and excise, and transport in Gujarat. In the villages of Gujarat, Modi and Shah identified grassroots leaders who felt alienated by the

Congress. They co-opted these disgruntled leaders and erected a parallel structure of institutionalized power. The same strategy was adopted to weaken the Congress's hold over Gujarat's influential cooperatives.

The 2014 general election was not the first time in India's electoral history that a political party won an impressive majority on its own in the Lok Sabha. But, for the first time, India had a prime minister who was deeply committed to an ideology, namely that harboured by the RSS. As prime minister, Modi seldom mentioned RSS ideologue M.S. Golwalkar but Golwalkar's thoughts and writings had a deep influence on him. As Manini Chatterjee wrote in her weekly column in the *Telegraph*, 'Narendra bhai Modi was the best vehicle to translate the RSS's vision into reality. Modi, a powerful orator, possessed of indefatigable energy, with his peerless grandstanding, bear-hugging every world leader within handshaking distance, had the ability to say things that were instantly believed by the masses regardless of factual accuracy or historical context.'

According to Chatterjee, the 2014 election marked a seminal moment in the dream of forming a Hindu *rashtra*. She pointed out that in his first major speech in the Lok Sabha after becoming prime minister Modi had referred to end '1200 years of foreign rule'. As if to bear this out, the period between 2014 and 2017 saw a sudden spurt of violence against minorities and Dalits in the guise of *ghar wapsi*, 'love jihad' and cow vigilantism. While the RSS and the BJP often condemned these acts as the handiwork of the 'loony fringe', commentators like Chatterjee were clear that these events were rooted in the ideological sustenance of the RSS and inspired by the writings of right-wing ideologue M.S. Golwalkar. To quote Chatterjee, 'Deendayal Upadhyaya displacing Nehru is only a curtain-raiser. Golwalkar, the *Manusmriti* and the Bhagwa Dhwaj wait in the wings – to replace Mahatma Gandhi, the Constitution and the Tricolour.'

However, in his three years in office, Brand Modi has taken a beating due to growing unemployment, economic slowdown, hardships faced by the general populace during the demonetization exercise of 2016 (with no apparent benefit in regards to eradication of black money visible), the unforeseen complications caused by the introduction of nation-wide Goods and Services Tax (GST), bad governance in several party ruled states like Haryana, Rajasthan, Jharkhand, Madhya Pradesh and little headway in normalization of the situation in Jammu and Kashmir. Modi's pet projects such as

Make in India and Digital India have also suffered due to a lack of clarity in policies and infrastructural bottlenecks.

Yet, Brand Modi is far from being considered weak and debates rage on about the turn the 2019 general election will take. While it would seem that Modi, with his promises of development, employment and education (which do not seem to be close to getting fulfilled), still has the power to draw in the votes, there are no absolutes in Indian democracy. After all, in the recent election held in Modi's home state Gujarat, even in defeat, it was Rahul Gandhi who was praised for his efforts and spoken of as finally having come into his own.

7

A MESSIAH OF THE MASSES

AS THE DANCE OF DEMOCRACY CONTINUED IN POST-Independent India, several significant trends emerged. On 5 April 1957, E.M. Nambudripad, the leader of the Kerala Legislature Communist Party took over as the state's chief minister after defeating the Congress in the assembly election. This was the first time that a communist government was elected to power anywhere in the world. Ten years later, the domination of a single political party – the Congress – began to show signs of decline. Regional parties and communities began to challenge the Congress and a number of regional parties headed or fronted by charismatic individuals began to dominate the political scene. Regionalism, a plethora of political parties representing particular community identities and varied socio-economic interests became part and parcel of the country's politics. State elections across the country began to deliver verdicts that not only had a crucial bearing on the nation's politics and governance, but also brought into focus the emergence of powerful – and often colourful characters – who impacted polity. There are too many such stories to narrate, but a few state polls that not only proved to be turning points in the political journey of a particular state but also introduced larger-than-life regional satraps are certainly worthy of discussion. One such is the election in 1983 that brought to power actor-turned-politician N.T. Rama Rao in what was then the state of Andhra Pradesh.

Andhra Pradesh came into existence following the revolutionary freedom fighter Potti Sreeramulu's fast unto death, demanding that a separate Telugu state be carved out of the Telugu-speaking districts of Madras State and Hyderabad State. From the state's inception in the 1950s to 1983, the Indian National Congress won every assembly election held in the state.

Things changed for the state after 1982, triggered by an unusual occurrence. In 1982, Rajiv Gandhi, then the AICC general secretary, visited Andhra Pradesh on a 'private' visit. At the Begumpet airport, the otherwise sober Rajiv lost his temper when he spotted Congress Chief Minister Tanguturi

Anjaiah waiting to welcome him, armed with garlands, his entire cabinet in attendance. The pomp and ceremony, and the crowd of party workers continued as the chief minister failed to read Rajiv's angry reaction. At the end of it, those within hearing distance heard Rajiv calling Anjaiah, an elderly politician hailing from a weaker section of society, a 'buffoon'. Rajiv's arrogance and rashness did not end there. Back in Delhi, he convinced Indira Gandhi to sack Anjaiah. While giving up his post, Anjaiah is reported to have remarked that he came to power by the 'grace of Madam' and he was leaving under her orders, but he did not know why he had come or why he had to leave. This perceived insult to a 'Telugu *bidda*' became welcome ammunition for N.T. Rama Rao, newly arrived on the political scene, and in the 1983 state assembly polls his Telugu Desam Party (TDP) stormed to power, fighting for *atmagauravam* (self-respect).

N.T. Rama Rao, popularly known as NTR, had turned 60 in 1982. A veteran of 292 films released between 1949 and 1982, NTR built up the TDP with the help of N. Chandrababu Naidu, his son-in-law and a minister in Anjaiah's cabinet. NTR began his campaign six months before voting was scheduled to begin, travelling across the state, covering over 75,000 kilometres and drawing unprecedented crowds. NTR ensured that the news of the formation of his political persona was seen and heard of by over thirty million people – this in a time before 24x7 news and social media became easy vehicles of the dissemination of news.

In some ways, NTR could be given credit for redefining the concept of election campaigning, creating methods that were later perfected by L.K. Advani and Narendra Modi – he converted a Chevrolet van into a *rath* (chariot), bringing tinsel-town techniques to politics. NTR's contemporaries and rivals, however, remained contemptuous of his innovative techniques, dismissing them as fads. Today, all politicians swear by the effectiveness of road shows. His vehicle, which he christened the 'Chaitanya Ratham', was fitted with rotating floodlights and loudspeakers. The actor would climb on to its top through a hatch to address amassed crowds and use the van's interior to relax. On average, he clocked 120 kilometres every day, stopping to address gatherings of 15 people and more. The Telugu press was in a tizzy. *Eenadu*, one of the state's largest-selling newspapers, was already on board with its owner Ramaji Rao becoming a staunch supporter of NTR. Each day, *Eenadu* would carry a story on how NTR had stopped by at a roadside shop to have a plate of piping hot *idli*s, *pesarattu* and coffee. The TDP even had a signature tune 'Maa Telugu thalliki malle poodanda', or 'a garland of jasmine flowers for Mother Telugu'. The response to the exhaustive tour was overwhelming. Even if NTR was late to arrive at his scheduled stop by 24 hours, and sometimes even 72 hours, he would find throngs of people waiting. They would camp right by the roadside, bringing along cots, stoves and utensils, to ensure they did not miss him. Dasu Keshav Rao of *The Hindu* remembers NTR being so focused on winning the 1983 assembly polls that he did not return to Hyderabad until the election was announced, missing the marriage ceremonies of two of his sons as a result.

On the campaign trail, NTR focused on the Congress government's corruption and decay and the tendency of 'Delhi' – the central government – to use chief ministers like puppets. When Indira Gandhi travelled to Andhra Pradesh to campaign for the Congress, she realized that the party had no chance against NTR. Most Congress MLAs had not nursed their assembly constituencies, hoping that 'Indira *amma*'s' charisma would see them through. NTR, on the other hand, had done his homework well. Aided by a young and crafty Naidu, the TDP chose as their representatives educated people from various walks of life, with clean images and a desire to serve in public life. NTR also tried making strategic pre-poll alliances with non-Congress players such as the Left parties, the Janata Party and the Sanjay Vichar Manch led by Maneka Gandhi. However, by the time the assembly polls were held, only Maneka's party was still on board as the Left grossly underestimated NTR's appeal and demanded 150 out of 294 seats. Both NTR and Naidu were clear that the TDP would contest the majority of seats to enable the party to form a government on its own strength.

Among NTR's election promises one was to make rice available for the people at ₹2 for a kilogram. In those days, the union government had classified rice into three categories – common, fine and super fine. Their market prices were ₹2.50 for the common variety, and ₹2.80 for the fine and super fine varieties. NTR promised the people that all varieties of rice would be available to them at ₹2 for a kilogram. Although he was derided by the Congress, the voters took him up on his offer.

In the end, the TDP won 201 out of 290 seats while the Congress finished with 60 seats, and NTR became the first non-Congress chief minister of Andhra Pradesh.

Both Indira and Rajiv were deeply upset over

the Congress's defeat in Andhra Pradesh and took NTR's success as a personal setback. In 1984, when NTR was away in the United States for a medical procedure, Governor Ram Lal, under instructions from the Centre, dismissed NTR's government, despite their being in the majority. The Congress propped up a TDP rebel, N. Bhaskara Rao, as the chief minister. The unjustified dismissal was decried by 17 Opposition parties in the state, including the CPI (M), BJP, National Conference, DMK and the Janata Party. NTR rushed back and took charge of the situation. He took to wearing black all the time to register his protest. He paraded his party's MLAs outside Rashtrapati Bhawan to demonstrate the support his government enjoyed. As a result of the furore caused by the Centre's interference in the state's governance, Bhaskara Rao lasted for merely 31 days as chief minister and NTR was reinstated.

The situation created in Andhra Pradesh was but one of many that cropped up during Indira Gandhi's prime ministerial tenure. The first United Front government in West Bengal, comprising Jyoti Basu's CPI (M), the CPI and the Bangla Congress, was formed in March 1967 but was dismissed within eight months. The dismissal was executed controversially by the then Governor Dharma

Vira whose appointment had been opposed by the Left. In November 1967, Vira rejected Basu's majority claim without putting it to a test and President's Rule was imposed. In Tamil Nadu, M. Karunanidhi's government was dismissed on 31 January 1976 by the Centre after the DMK leader openly challenged the imposition of the Emergency in 1975.

Rajiv Gandhi's years as prime minister also saw several state governments, from Kashmir to Karnataka, being toppled by the Centre. Rajiv's home minister Buta Singh was known as Rajiv's 'axe man'. Between 1985 and 1989, while serving as the Union home minister, he toppled so many state governments that Rajiv is said to have told him in jest, '*Buta Singhji, ab aap kirpan andar rakhiye*' (Buta Singhji, now please sheath your *kirpan*).

It would take a landmark Supreme Court verdict in 1994 to end the arbitrary use of Article 356 of the Indian Constitution, which allowed the Centre to dismiss state governments. While issuing the judgement – called the 'Bommai judgement' after S.R. Bommai, the Karnataka chief minister, whose government was dismissed by the Centre before President's Rule – the apex court also issued strict guidelines on the imposition of President's Rule in a state by the Centre.

Once back as chief minister, NTR introduced several populist welfare measures, cementing his place in the hearts of the Telugu-speaking population. While he zealously emphasized Telugu culture and language, according to his biographer S. Venkat, his lesser-known achievement was to have convinced Indira how economically and politically strong Indian states could ensure a strong Centre, contradicting her earlier notion that strong states implied a weak Centre. He was the first to take up the cause of amendments in the Hindu Succession Act to ensure equal property rights for women. NTR also introduced educational reforms and laid the foundation for the Telugu Ganga project to provide drinking water to Madras (now Chennai) city and to irrigate the dry lands of Rayalaseema.

NTR's bond with Andhra Pradesh strengthened to such an extent that in the 1984–85 Lok Sabha polls, held after Indira Gandhi's assassination, the Congress won 414 out of 533 seats in the Lok Sabha, a 77 per cent majority, but failed to capitalize on the 'sympathy vote' in Andhra Pradesh. Out of the 42 Lok Sabha seats from the state, they could win only 6. The TDP won 30 parliamentary seats making it the principal Opposition party in the Lok Sabha. This was a stunning reversal in a state that had even in the post-Emergency 1977 election voted for the Congress in 41 out of 42 seats.

By this time, there was no dearth of people advocating that NTR should take to national politics. By 1987, Rajiv Gandhi's 'Mr Clean' image had taken a beating from scandals such as the Bofors arms deal and the Shah Bano case and the 1989 general election saw the National Front, a combine of several anti-Congress parties, come to power at the Centre with the support of the BJP and the Left Front. NTR was a key player in the National Front and the government at the Centre helmed by V.P. Singh. However, amidst a growing feeling among his followers that he had begun to neglect Andhra Pradesh, the Congress captured power in the state in 1989, pushing NTR to the Opposition benches. NTR bounced back in 1994, despite a fellow Telugu *bidda* P.V. Narasimha Rao being prime minister of India at that time, but his reign was soon to end in a dramatic manner.

Nine months into his third term as the chief minister of Andhra Pradesh, on 26 August 1995, his son-in-law and trusted lieutenant Chandrababu Naidu staged a coup. Naidu attributed the revolt against NTR to the vice-like grip that Lakshmi Parvathi, NTR's second wife, increasingly had on NTR and his political affairs and decisions. Virtually all the members of his family and 200 TDP legislators supported Naidu, deserting the chief minister and reducing him to nothing.

In his 2009 book *The Other Side of Truth*, NTR's other son-in-law, Venkateshwara Rao, claimed that NTR was so enraged by Naidu's revolt that he asked his son Balakrishna to murder Naidu and show him the 'sword stained with Naidu's blood'. Rao recalled how, on 26 August 1995, he was surrounded by around 40 TDP MLAs when he landed at Begumpet Airport, and was taken to the Viceroy Hotel, where Naidu told him about the coup. Despite his wife supporting her father, Rao sided with Naidu, though he later called it an 'unforgivable sin'. Rao returned to NTR's camp a fortnight later and stayed with him till the actor's death. NTR died a disillusioned man, in January 1996, allegedly for want of good medical care.

Naidu's own version of the events of August 1995 came 16 years later in 2011, when he told scribes in Hyderabad that he had to revolt to save the TDP party and Andhra Pradesh. Claiming that Lakshmi's influence was threatening the TDP, Naidu added that they had tried all possible means of checking her influence and saving the party but failed and, left with no option, had been compelled to effect a leadership change and form the government in a democratic manner with the support of more than 200 MLAs.

The TDP, under Naidu, retained power till 2004, when the Congress under Y.S. Rajasekhara Reddy formed the government. In 2014, the state was bifurcated into Andhra Pradesh and Telangana, comprising the Telugu-speaking districts of the erstwhile Hyderabad state, the culmination of a decade-long agitation. The Congress, which had seen this reorganization through, gained nothing electorally, however, winning only 2 seats in the 2014 general election. In the 2014 assembly election, the TDP won over a hundred of the 180 seats in the Andhra Pradesh assembly, and Chandrababu Naidu became the first chief minister of this 'new' bifurcated state.

8

THE TIGER ROARS IN MAHARASHTRA

WHILE N.T. RAMA RAO, USED HIS CHARM AND CHARISMA to become an elected leader, Balasaheb Thackeray was in a league of his own, wielding extreme power without ever becoming an elected representative. For over three decades, Thackeray dominated politics, business and even Bollywood in such a manner that the Shiv Sena's electoral forays paled in comparison to the rise of a 'Tiger'.

On 14 March 1995, after having lost Uttar Pradesh, Bihar, Tamil Nadu, Bengal and Andhra Pradesh, the Congress lost its last big citadel, handing over the reins of the Maharashtra state government to a Shiv Sena–BJP combine. The Shiv Sena in Mumbai was known particularly for its aggression, unruly behaviour and violent campaigns against communists, Muslims and migrant populations from northern and southern Indian states and

Bihar residing in the metropolitan city. Accused of instigating major riots in Maharashtra over time, including those that tore Mumbai apart in the late 1960s and again in 1992 and 1993, and the Bhiwandi riots of 1984, the Sena was a proud practitioner of its radical Hindutva ideology laced with parochial objectives.

The Sena's founder Balasaheb Thackeray, a Marathi-speaking Kayastha from Madhya Pradesh, had nothing to do with the RSS, the Jan Sangh, the Hindu Mahasabha or the Vishwa Hindu Parishad. Thackeray formed the Shiv Sena in 1966 at the age of 40 when he was working as a cartoonist in the *Free Press Journal* in Mumbai. (This was a time when migrants from south Indian states, particularly Tamil Nadu, were calling the shots in the metropolis and many Marathi-speaking youth – the 'sons of the soil' – were unable to find employment. Simultaneously, communists and labour unions dominated on the political front.)

Thackeray, whose cartooning style was influenced by David Low, was reportedly denied a promotion allegedly by a 'South Indian clique'. He left his job to start a political weekly called *Marmik*, which culminated in the launch of the Shiv Sena. He used *Marmik* as a satirical vehicle of protest, highlighting the recruitment of non-Maharashtrians in both government and private industries under the headline, '*Vaacha ani gappa basa*', or 'Read and be quiet'. Soon, South Indians residing in Mumbai were targeted with the war cry '*Bajao pungi, bhagao lungi*', which was coined by Thackeray himself.

On 1 May 1966, an editorial in *Marmik* decried the Maharashtra government's support for industries whose owners recruited labourers from outside Maharashtra, questioning the rightness of creating employment for migrants while locals remained unemployed. In the same issue of the magazine, Thackeray published a list of officers at a government-owned fertilizer company, which showed that only three officers employed there were from Maharashtra while the rest were from other states. He called it an insult to Maharashtra.

Journalist and author Vir Sanghvi, who interacted with Thackeray from close quarters, has been quoted as saying that Thackeray was 'the biggest Bollywood showman of his era' – much bigger than Raj Kapoor, Amitabh Bachchan or Rajesh Khanna. Sanghvi called him a 'born actor' who knew how to be funny, smart, sardonic and then suddenly inspiring. According to journalist and commentator Kumar Ketkar, the Shiv Sena has no ideology as such. In an article on the party, Ketkar contended that the Sena was born on the streets of Mumbai, and thrived on mindless actions. Ketkar further stated that Thackeray disdained the trappings of power and never wanted the responsibility that came with power.

Thackeray's rise is also a telling commentary on how the Congress, which excelled in propping up regional players to settle its own regional satraps, paid the price for its Machiavellian designs. In the Sena's initial years, the Congress used and manipulated Thackeray and his nascent party to 'fix' Morarji Desai, Krishna Menon and a number of others who were opposed to Indira Gandhi.

In her biography of Thackeray, *Hindu Hriday Samrat: How the Shiv Sena Changed Mumbai Forever*, author Sujata Anandan has meticulously recorded how the Shiv Sena was then derogatorily referred to as the 'Vasant Sena' after the veteran Congress leaders Vasantrao Naik and Vasantdada Patil gave the Sena credibility by accepting its demand of 80 per cent employment of locals in business establishments. Both Naik and Patil detested the dominance of Gujarati, Parsi, Sindhi and Bohra Muslim enterprises in Mumbai and Maharashtra, and used the Sena's vociferous demands to their advantage. From that time on, Thackeray played his role as the Congress's hit man till, like Jarnail Singh

Bhindranwale in mid-1980s Punjab, he became a cult figure with his own following.

One election where the Shiv Sena helped out the Congress was the 1967 Lok Sabha election. Congress stalwart V.K. Krishna Menon had been denied a party ticket and was contesting as an independent candidate from the Bombay North East constituency. His campaign was based entirely on his proximity to Jawaharlal Nehru. The posters for his campaign read 'Nehru's vision, Menon's mission' and showed an image of Menon placed within Nehru's silhouette. Indira Gandhi, who was fighting to isolate Menon, instructed her key aides to get the former defence minister defeated at 'all costs'. Following this, Thackeray, the Shiv Sena and *Marmik* swung into action, campaigning for the Congress nominee in the constituency, S.G. Barve. A day before the votes, *Marmik* published a cartoon that showed Menon with his hands around the shoulders of two foreign girls. The caption insinuated that they were the main motivation behind Menon's desire to be defence minister. With Menon thus discredited in the eyes of voters, Barve won the election quite easily.

Thackeray had a brush with the law in February 1969, when he was arrested for starting a riot. When Morarji Desai, then deputy prime minister

and former chief minister of undivided Bombay State, visited the metropolis, Sena workers had tried to stop Morarji Desai's car at Mahim to hand him a memorandum demanding the merger of Belgaum, Karwar and Nipani in Maharashtra. Desai's driver panicked in the face of the gathering crowd and drove off quickly, injuring several *sainik*s in the process. Angry *sainik*s began rioting and the violence lasted for four days. The Congress chief minister of the state, Vasantrao Naik, did little to check the Sena rioters, leading to massive destruction of life and property. The situation deteriorated to the extent that the army had to be called in. Sixty-nine people died in the agitation. Thackeray and his party colleagues, Manohar Joshi and Dattaji Salvi, were arrested and sent to Yerwada Central Jail in Pune and later to Arthur Road Jail in Mumbai, but they were released after 100 days by the Congress government reportedly due to 'instructions from the top'.

In September 1970, the Sena tasted its first significant victory, riding on support from the RSS. Krishna Desai, a communist MLA from Parel, a Bombay suburb, was murdered, necessitating a by-election. The Sena fielded Vaman Mahadik in the by-election while the communists put the late Desai's wife Sarojini in the fray. Nine political parties including the Congress supported Sarojini. Comrade S. Dange and senior Congress leaders such as Mohan Dharia and Shankarrao Chavan campaigned for her but the Sena won the seat, with RSS leader Moropant Pingale publicly appealing to the people to vote for the Sena.

When Indira Gandhi declared a national emergency on the country in 1975, Thackeray supported it whole-heartedly. In an editorial in *Marmik* on 31 August 1975, he wrote that imposing an emergency was the only way to handle the situation created after widespread unrest, but he cautioned against prolonging it.

In the 1980 assembly election, the Sena did not field any candidates against the Congress. Abdul Rahman Antulay, a personal friend of Thackeray, served as the Congress chief minister from 1980 to 1982. During his tenure, Antulay promised with nationalistic zeal to bring the Maratha warrior-king Chhatrapati Shivaji Maharaj's legendary 'Bhavani' sword back from the United Kingdom, where it was believed to be housed at the British Museum. The request, moved through the Indian Mission in London, resulted in Antulay getting an appointment with Her Majesty the Queen of England, but he was unseated before his London visit over a controversy about granting cement quotas. Later, as a minister in Narasimha Rao's cabinet in the 1990s, Antulay stunned Congressmen by declaring himself a 'Shiv Sainik' and urged an interviewer not to address him as 'Abdul Rahman', clarifying that he preferred to be called A.R. Antulay as it camouflaged his religious identity.

The irascible and whimsical Thackeray would often become 'soft' on the Congress on some pretext or the other. The Sena chief supported the Congress's presidential nominee in 2007 on the grounds of contender Pratibha Patil being a 'Marathi manus', and in 2012 he backed Pranab Mukherjee, describing the veteran leader as 'a deserving candidate'.

Unlike most politicians and party supremos, Thackeray neither held public office nor contested an election. He did, however, create a dubious legacy for himself by getting disenfranchised. It started with Congress politician Prabhakar Kunte filing a case in the Bombay High Court accusing Ramesh Prabhoo of the Shiv Sena of corrupt electoral practices after losing a by-election to the state assembly to Prabhoo in 1986 for the Vile Parle constituency in Bombay North-West. The matter moved to the Supreme Court, which convicted Thackeray for corrupt electoral practices and advised the President of India to debar him from contesting or voting in elections for a period of six years. Subsequently, the Election Commission debarred him from contesting any election or exercising his right to vote from 1995 to 2001, and Maharashtra Chief Electoral Officer D. K. Sankaran ordered the deletion of Thackeray's name from the voters' list in Bombay. While Thackeray made light of his disenfranchisement, it was a victory for Kunte.

Thackeray's biggest moment in politics came when he struck an alliance with the BJP in 1995 and formed a government in the state for the first time, tempering his strident pro-Marathi ideology and embracing a broader Hindu nationalist agenda. Much of the credit for bringing the Sena and BJP together was given to BJP's Pramod Mahajan, a fellow Maharashtrian who enjoyed Thackeray's trust. Mahajan was an astute politician who knew that a Hindutva agenda and a strong alliance with the Shiv Sena was the only way that the BJP would rule Maharashtra.

The Sena–BJP combine also owed its political success to the 1993 Mumbai serial bomb blasts and the communal riots that followed, which polarized voters to their advantage. A judicial commission, headed by Justice B.N. Srikrishna, which had probed the riots, had squarely accused Thackeray of sparking anti-Muslim violence in Mumbai, which claimed over 1,000 lives. Justice Srikrishna, himself a devout Hindu, described Thackeray as a 'veteran general who commanded his loyal Shiv Sainiks to retaliate by organized attacks against Muslims' during the riots.

Thackeray often described himself as the 'remote control' running the Manohar Joshi-led Sena–BJP regime of 1995–2000. Thackeray showed his power over Chief Minister Joshi within days of the Sena–BJP coming to power at a party organized for a select few in Mumbai to celebrate the Sena–BJP victory. When Thackeray walked in, he was dismayed to note that liquor was not being served. On being told that liquor was not supposed to flow in the presence of the chief minister, Thackeray lost his temper and immediately ordered for champagne to be brought. A sheepish Joshi moved to a corner to avoid being photographed amidst alcohol-induced revelry. But Thackeray's influence affected far more serious matters. On the floor of the Maharashtra Assembly, Thackeray pressured Chief Minister Joshi to reject the findings of the Srikrishna Commission investigating the perpetrators of the Mumbai riots. The Sena chief not only rubbished the findings, but also cast aspersions on the integrity of the presiding judge.

For the next four years, Joshi carefully served to project the Sena as a responsible party of governance, until Thackeray had him removed just before the March 2000 state assembly polls. Joshi was in Pune on 30 January 1999, meeting Marathi literary figures involved in a writers' conference. When he returned to Mumbai late in the afternoon, he found a fax message from Thackeray waiting for him, asking him to step down. Joshi called up Thackeray to assure him that his demand would be honoured and his removal was effected with ease.

Joshi's successor was Narayan Tatu Rane, who pushed aggressively for communal mobilization of masses but his actions failed and the Sena–BJP combine lost the state assembly polls in September 1999 to the Congress. The Congress's rise to power, however, was not without hiccups and compromise. In May 1999, Sharad Pawar revolted against Sonia Gandhi on the grounds of her foreign origin and was thrown out of the party. Pawar formed the breakaway party, Nationalist Congress Party (NCP), and campaigned extensively against the Congress. But the 1999 assembly polls resulted in a fractured mandate in which Sena won 69 assembly seats while its ally, the BJP, won 56 in a house of 288. The Congress emerged as the single-largest party with 75 MLAs. A crafty Pawar did not waste time in joining hands with the Congress once again as his NCP had already won 58 assembly seats. Rane, too, subsequently joined the Congress and then, in 2017, switched over once again to the BJP.

The influence of the Shiv Sena chief was also prominently visible in the Mumbai film industry. He was friends with and respected by the who's who of Hindi cinema and his love for films was well known. But this relationship too suffered from its share of conflicts and controversies. In 1998, Thackeray went berserk when the government of Pakistan conferred the Nishan-e-Imtiaz, their highest civilian award, on Dilip Kumar, his long-time friend, and objected to his going to Pakistan to receive it. This kicked off a massive political row. Dilip Kumar said at the time that what had upset him most was that his cartoonist-turned-politician friend of three decades had cast doubts on his patriotism. Eventually, Dilip Kumar travelled to Pakistan and was accompanied by Sunil Dutt, where he was presented the award by the then Pakistan President Rafiq Tarar during the Pakistan Day ceremony in Islamabad on 23 March 1998.

By November 2012, had caught up to a man whose charisma had made him seem tireless and Thackeray's health began to fail. At the Sena's Dussehra rally held on 24 October 2012, the tiger's roar was missing. In a video-recorded address, Thackeray virtually announced his retirement from public life and urged his followers to stand by his son Uddhav and his grandson Aditya, setting out the succession plan in the Shiv Sena. (Thackeray's nephew Raj had parted ways with him in 2006 to form a more hawkish party, the Maharashtra Nirman Sena (MNS), owing to a feud between him and Uddhav.)

When Thackeray died on 17 November 2012, his body was kept at Shivaji Park in central Mumbai for people to pay their last respects. Movie theatres, shops and commercial establishments throughout Mumbai remained closed for two days. A state funeral, which entails taking the deceased's body draped in the Tricolour in a procession on a gun-carriage with police or army escorts, besides a 21-gun salute ahead of the funeral, is an honour reserved for those who have held constitutional posts such as prime ministerships, but the Congress chief minister of Maharashtra at the time, Prithviraj Chavan, ordered one for Thackeray, disregarding murmurs from within the Congress and dismissing criticism by saying he was responding to the 'public sentiment'. Thus, in death Thackeray achieved the state honour that had missed him in his lifetime.

After Bal Thackeray's death, the Shiv Sena has faced many difficulties. The biggest challenge came when Narendra Modi–Amit Shah combine led the BJP to gain an upper hand in Mumbai as well as in pockets across Maharashtra, increasingly winning more seats in the civic, assembly and Lok Sabha polls. The Shiv Sena could not muster enough courage to part ways with the BJP, and instead of finding its own footing grumbled and sulked about perceived slights. The character and firepower that the Sena had assumed under Thackeray's leadership went missing under Thackeray's son Uddhav. While the Sena continued to champion the politics of language and regional interests, the party lost the core theme of Hindutva to the BJP.

Uddhav did not inspire Sena activists the way Thackeray had, though he was successful in keeping cousin Raj under check. Uddhav's achievement of scoring over NCP and MNS was somewhat lost in the ascent of the BJP in Maharashtra, and in this sense the Sena faces a grim future. Thackeray had, it seems, thrived on the politics of hate, regardless of whether he was targeting South Indians, Gujaratis or Muslims. Towards the later part of his life, his vitriolic attacks became more specifically directed towards Pakistan. He favoured strong-arm tactics to voice his animosity, often forcing central and state governments to call off cricket matches with Pakistan and performances by Pakistani artistes. Under his direction, in October 1991, Shiv Sainiks dug up the Wankhede Stadium's pitch to prevent the Pakistan cricket team from playing in Mumbai, and the Narasimha Rao government then ruling at the Centre and the Board of Control for Cricket in India (BCCI) were forced to call off the series. Other such instances of disruption followed in 1999 and 2005.

Many have wondered how Thackeray was able to mobilize the youth so easily. His real strength was his ability to recognize the presence of a large number of unemployed youth whose frustrations drove them to indulge in violence at the slightest provocation, and providing them with situations that allowed them to vent their anger as well as the assurance that they would be bailed out if the law got to them. Thackeray always told Shiv Sainiks not to read. He was dismissive of all social, political and economic theories and instructed his followers not to heed such bunkum.

Later in his life, Thackeray avoided mingling with supporters and made up for it by giving occasional grand '*darshans*' from the balcony of his heavily guarded Bandra home 'Matoshree' and giving rabble-rousing speeches at his famous

Dussehra rallies. Seated on a throne and surrounded by multiple images of a tiger, Thackeray virtually lorded over Mumbai for years, receiving political leaders, captains of business and industry, and film personalities at his residence, all without holding an official position of power.

9

BAHUJAN KI BEHENJI

ON 11 MAY 2007, AT THE PRERNA STHAL TEMPLE INSIDE the headquarters of the Bahujan Samaj Party (BSP) in Lucknow, Mayawati stood in silence for a minute before three tall stone statues – those of B.R. Ambedkar, Kanshi Ram and herself. The story goes that as she stepped out of the temple it began to rain, and her followers, who had until then been sweating in the intense summer heat, interpreted the sudden shower as 'divine approval' being bestowed upon the change of guard in Uttar Pradesh. Mayawati's ascent to power in India's most populous and politically significant state had been achieved through sweat and toil and a long-time commitment to the Dalit cause. Remarkably, she was also the first-ever chief minister of Uttar Pradesh to complete a term in office – a feat that had eluded many an illustrious leader for six decades before her.

By 2007, Uttar Pradesh had seen over 30 chief ministers come and go – stalwarts such as Pandit Govind Ballabh Pant, Kamalapati Tripathi, Sampurnanand, Sucheta Kriplani, Narain Dutt Tiwari, Mulayam Singh Yadav and Kalyan Singh – but not a single one among them completed a full term in office. In fact, a roll call of Uttar Pradesh's chief ministers would turn out to be an endless affair. Even Pant, a legendary figure and freedom fighter, whose political skills were highly regarded by both Mahatma Gandhi and Jawaharlal Nehru, could not achieve this feat. He served as chief minister four times – twice before Independence and twice after – but his stints were separated by assembly polls and then by his appointment as the country's home minister in December 1954.

Sampurnanand, a teacher and a key participant in the freedom struggle, who succeeded Pant, served as chief minister from December 1954 to December 1960, his tenure interrupted by the April 1957 assembly polls. Sampurnanand's successor, Chandra Bhanu Gupta, was a consummate politician, but of his three stints in office only the first lasted for more than two years. Sucheta Kriplani, the successor of Gupta's first term and the predecessor of his second, spent three years in office (1963–1967), and when Gupta returned to office on 14 March 1967, he couldn't survive beyond 18 days. His uneasy ties with Indira Gandhi and attempts at one-upmanship with Kamalapati Tripathi and Hemvati Nandan Bahuguna resulted in political instability. This is believed to be among the biggest reasons for the emergence of the first non-Congress government in the heartland, with the rebel Congress leader Chaudhary Charan Singh forming the government in 1967 under the banner of his newly formed political party – Bhartiya Kranti Dal.

Through the 1970s, governments were formed by various political parties with different ideologies – Charan Singh, Tribhuvan Narain Singh, H.N. Bahuguna, N.D. Tiwari, Ram Naresh Yadav and Banarasi Das to name a few – and just as easily collapsed. This paved the way for multiple spells of President's Rule being imposed on the state. Vir Bahadur Singh next headed the Congress government in UP between September 1985 and June 1988. The state was then handed over to N.D. Tiwari, who took up the job for the third time. Tiwari has the dubious honour of being the last Congress chief minister of an undivided Uttar Pradesh.

In December 1989, Samajwadi Party's (SP) leader

Mulayam Singh Yadav worked out a deal with the Congress to become chief minister, but the June 1991 polls saw a resurgent BJP win the election. The BJP rule, too, did not last and 6 December 1992 marked the dismissal of Kalyan Singh who had been the BJP's chosen chief minister.

Continuing the revolving-door kind of situation at the chief minister's office, the 1990s saw the short-lived alliance of Mulayam Singh and Mayawati under a Kanshi Ram-supervised power-share formula and the BJP's rule between 1997 and 2002, which had Kalyan Singh, Ram Prakash Gupta and Rajnath Singh occupy the chair. Eventually, it was Mulayam Singh's tenure from August 2003 to May 2007 that provided the state with some degree of stability.

It was in May 2007 that history was created when Mayawati defied her critics and won a decisive mandate. The support that she received from the Brahmin, Dalit and Muslim communities alike humbled arch-rival Mulayam Singh Yadav, defused Rahul Gandhi's spirited campaign and kept the BJP at bay. Mayawati's performance was deemed worthy of her party's symbol, the elephant, as the Bahujan Samaj Party (BSP) romped home with 206 seats, four more than the number required to form a government in the state.

Mayawati's swearing-in ceremony at Raj Bhawan in Lucknow presented an interesting tableau. Her parents, Ramlata and Prabhu Das, could be seen sitting in awestruck silence, watching 49 BSP ministers bow before their daughter and touch her feet. Among them were those who were so overwhelmed at being in Mayawati's presence, it seemed as if they were trembling and could barely read the oath. But not once during the hour-long ceremony did Mayawati turn and look at her parents. When they finally came face-to-face with her after the proceedings, she mechanically introduced them to Governor T.V. Rajeswar. Ramlata and Prabhu Das hesitantly bowed before the Governor but Mayawati still looked distant, making no eye contact with them.

BSP leaders claimed that making any gesture of affection or reverence towards them would have been 'too Manuvadi' for her comfort.

In 2005, Mayawati had officially announced at the BSP headquarters that she would be snapping relations with her parents so that she could dedicate herself to the cause of Dalit empowerment. Her parents had accepted her decision as some kind of divine command. Since that day, Mayawati had 'ceased' to be their daughter. Like the rest of the Bahujan Samaj, they too started calling her

'*Behenji*'. It is this kind of dedication to her cause that has seen Mayawati rise to the top.

In fact, 2007 was not the first time that Mayawati became the chief minister. In June 1995, she had taken oath as the head of a coalition government. At that time, Prime Minister P.V. Narasimha Rao had been in France and, while addressing captains of trade and industry in Paris, had described Mayawati as a 'miracle of democracy'. He had marvelled at how a woman hailing from one of the most neglected sections of Indian society had assumed the powerful office of chief minister.

Born as Mayawati Prabhu Das on 15 January 1956, Mayawati has led an extraordinary and inspirational life. She spent her early years at Badalpur, Noida, where her father was an employee in the postal department and often struggled to pay the ₹15 tuition fee for his children who studied at a local government school. Her life remained mundane and tough till she graduated from Delhi's Kalindi College, acquired a law and a B.Ed. degree and settled for a school-teacher's job in Ghaziabad. Mayawati was preparing for the Civil Services examination while supporting her family through her teaching job when Kanshi Ram spotted her. This was around the year 1977. Little did she know then that under his guidance she would go on to become an icon for her community, Uttar Pradesh's chief minister on four occasions and the highest tax payer in the country.

Kanshi Ram, who had founded the BSP in 1984, had devoted his entire life to the cause of India's downtrodden. He remained unmarried and vowed not to own any property, dedicating his time and resources to providing social justice for Dalits. He shunned the word 'Harijan', coined by Mahatma Gandhi for Dalits. To him the word 'Harijan' implied that Dalits were helpless orphans who needed God or 'Hari' to protect and nurture them.

A firm believer in political power as the key to all social progress, Kanshi Ram often redefined the rules of Indian politics. He was convinced that an unstable government at the federal and state levels was beneficial for the Bahujan Samaj Party, as that could help him to secure great advantages for the marginalized. He wanted a *mazboor*, or weak, government, he said, and not a *mazboot*, or strong, one till Dalits had reached the Centre.

Mayawati first contested the Lok Sabha election in 1984 from Kairana, Uttar Pradesh. That year, the Rajiv Gandhi-led Congress swept the polls. Next year, a by-election was held at Bijnor, where Mayawati again lost. In 1987, in another by-election at Hardwar, she improved her standing, finishing second. In 1989, Bijnor saw Mayawati entering the Parliament. Inside the Lok Sabha, Mayawati developed a reputation as someone with an acid tongue. She missed no opportunity to attack upper caste 'Manuvadi' colleagues and her utterances met the approval of Dalit voters who admired her courage, assertiveness and aggressiveness.

Opportunity knocked at Mayawati's door in 1993 when Kanshi Ram painstakingly worked out an alliance with the SP. Together, the SP and the BSP succeeded in overthrowing the BJP, which was riding high on their Hindutva plank after the demolition of the Babri Masjid. However, this power-sharing arrangement between the SP and BSP did not work for long and mutual suspicion, violence and allegations soon brought the government down. Both Mayawati and her mentor, Kanshi Ram, became pragmatic, and this time around teamed up with the BJP. In June 1995, Mayawati, the '*Dalit ki beti*', became chief minister with the support of the BJP. This ideologically mismatched alliance shocked critics and friends alike but Mayawati remained unfazed.

Between 1995 and 2003, the BSP allied with the BJP thrice and each time it grew at its partner's expense. Between 1996 and 2004, the BJP's Lok

Sabha tally from UP plunged from 52 (out of 84) seats for a vote share of 33 per cent to 10 (of 80) seats for a vote share of 22 per cent. Between 1996 and 2002, the party's seat share in the UP assembly declined from 174 (of 425) seats for 32.5 per cent to 88 (of 403) seats for 21 per cent.

Mayawati's success saw '*Behenji*' metamorphose into 'madame'. The BSP supremo was identified as owning 'disproportionate' assets and money. When the income tax sleuths came to investigate, they were given a list of one crore BSP workers who had reportedly contributed amounts of less than ₹20,000 each in cash towards the party.

Mayawati's rule in Uttar Pradesh saw the emergence of Dalit assertiveness and empowerment. The most significant and visible outcome of this was the way Uttar Pradesh's feudal social structure got neutralized. 'Socialist' and backward class leaders who had a history of subjugating the Dalits finally began paying attention to the 21 per cent voters. From the later part of the 1980s, Dalit voters started coming out in large numbers to cast their votes in 'Jat belts' of western Uttar Pradesh, where they once would not have been allowed to. In her brief tenures in 1995 and 1997, Mayawati rounded up 1,45,000 rowdies, criminals and goondas who were known to intimidate Dalits. Dalit women outnumbered the men in her public meetings and rallies, because they closely identified with Mayawati. However, in many areas such as judiciary and legal profession, Dalits remained highly under represented in spite of BSP's rule between 2007 and 2012. As per one estimate, there were barely 300–400 dalit lawyers practising from among over 10,000 lawyers at Allahabad high court.

Paradoxically, Mayawati's rule saw atrocities against Dalits increasing but activists explained this as a sign of Dalit assertion, as earlier Dalits who were being victimized could not muster the courage to approach the police or file complaints. On the flip side, Dalit writers such as Chandra Bhan, Badri Narayan, D.R. Darapuri and others felt that Mayawati's bid to court 'sarvjan' (upper castes) voters caused her to neglect the Dalit cause, which, in turn, weakened her political stature from 2012 onwards. After Mayawati's defeat in the February 2012 UP polls, Darapuri wrote, 'The main factors responsible for the decline in Mayawati's Dalit vote bank are her corruption, misgovernance, lack of development, neglect of Dalit atrocities and her autocratic stance. In an attempt to keep her sarvjan voters in good humour by neglecting Dalit atrocities, Mayawati [has] made the Dalits suffer doubly.'

In the 2014 Lok Sabha polls, the BJP had the last

laugh as the BSP drew a blank from UP while the BJP won 73 seats. In the 2017 UP assembly polls, the BSP tally was 19 seats, its worst performance since 1991, while the BJP virtually steamrolled its rivals with its tally of 312 seats. Several Dalit scholars termed the BSP's rout as the 'end of the road' for the party and its supremo. Dalit writer Kanwal Bharti commented that this humiliating defeat spelled Mayawati's last innings, that although she had saved the existence of the party, her game seemed to be over.

In July 2017, a somewhat miffed Mayawati resigned from the Rajya Sabha after she was not allowed to speak for more than three minutes on alleged atrocities against Dalits in the BJP-ruled UP. It is widely believed that the real reason for Mayawati's exit from the Rajya Sabha was that with her term ending in 2018 she was unlikely to return to the upper house and her goal for the moment was to prepare for the 2019 general election.

10

MA-MATI-MANUSH
MAMATA

FROM 1977 TO 2011, THE PEOPLE OF WEST BENGAL HAD consistently returned the Left Front to power. On 13 May 2011, when Mamata Banerjee finally 'liberated' Bengal from the world's longest democratically elected communist government, her victory was monumental enough to be remarked upon by the international media. She had, after all, gone from being an ordinary Congress worker to a powerful leader dwarfing other towering figures of Bengal politics such as Jyoti Basu, Bidhan Chandra Roy, Siddhartha Shankar Ray and Pranab Mukherjee.

The Left Front had come to power in Bengal following the end of the Emergency. Leftist parties in Bengal had been a part of previous governments in the state, such as the United Front's government between 1967 and 1971, and a part of various past coalitions as well. The Left Front, however, was a coalition of Leftist parties alone.

The Left Front's initial years in power were marked by some seminal legislation, such as Operation Barga, which gave share-croppers inheritable tenancy rights to the land they tilled, reorganization of the Panchayati system in the state, and legislation to strengthen workers' rights. These pro-people policies helped them win by massive margins in the elections that followed. Simultaneously, the Left Front also increased its control over the bureaucracy, academia and other facets of the state.

Mamata Banerjee first rose to prominence when Rajiv Gandhi appointed her as general secretary of the Indian Youth Congress, and in 1984, Mamata became a giant-killer when she humbled Somnath Chatterjee of the CPI (M), defeating him in the fight for the Jadavpur Lok Sabha seat. A defeat in 1989 from the same seat forced Mamata to shift to the Calcutta South seat, from where she has now been elected six times to Parliament.

Rajiv's assassination in 1991 left Mamata without a powerful patron. She was denied the office of Bengal Congress chief in spite of having the numerical strength in the intra-party polls. In 1991, her skull was fractured by a CPM goon Lalu Alam when she was leading a Congress rally in the southern part of Calcutta. Two years later, she was physically thrown out of Writers' Building, the Bengal state secretariat, by the police for protesting in front of the office of then chief minister Jyoti Basu. Both incidents had a deep impact on her and strengthened her resolve to throw out the Left Front from Bengal.

When Congress leaders tried to persuade Mamata to 'go slow' against the Left, she openly accused them (Sitaram Kesri, in particular) of behaving like a stooge of the CPM. This was when the Congress was supporting H.D. Deve Gowda's government at the Centre, of which the CPI was a part. Mamata became a rebel after her claim for a party post was denied yet again. She proposed a *mahajot*, or grand alliance, against the Left but the Congress leadership rejected it on the grounds that it would imply that the party was aligning itself with the right-wing BJP, which was a minor force in Bengal.

In 1997, Mamata left the Congress to form the All India Trinamool Congress, promising to end the CPM's rule, adopting the slogan, 'Now's the time', encapsulating a vision that had been illusory for years. But the events that unfolded in the years leading up to her big win in 2011 made it seem unlikely that she would ever topple the Left Front government. First, she fell out with the Congress because of P.V. Narasimha Rao, Sitaram Kesri and Sonia Gandhi's inability to give her a 'free hand' to take on the Left in Bengal. These Congress leaders relied more on Pranab Mukherjee than Mamata when it came to making strategic decisions about Bengal's politics, and Mukherjee was determined to see Mamata leave the Congress. (Mukherjee and Mamata may have subsequently bought peace, but events that followed stand as testimony to the Congress's error in not recognizing and acknowledging Mamata's leadership.) Then, in early 2001, Mamata walked out of the NDA cabinet and allied with the Congress for the state assembly election, but failed to register a win as the alliance won only 86 seats. In the 2004 Lok Sabha election, she was the only member of the Trinamool Congress to win a seat from Bengal. In 2006, the Trinamool Congress won only 30 seats in the state assembly election. On 4 August 2006, she hurled her resignation letter at the Deputy Speaker Charanjit Singh Atwal in the Lok Sabha as her adjournment motion on infiltration by Bangladeshis in Bengal was not allowed.

After the liberalization of the Indian economy in

1991, the dichotomy of a communist government democratically elected in a capitalist economy had become more apparent. After 2000, the Left Front increased its efforts to woo private capital to the state. The government made an attempt to acquire land to set up an SEZ in Nandigram in the district of East Midnapore, and began the process of getting Indonesia's Salim Group to set up a chemical hub there. Mamata launched a campaign to stop this chemical hub from coming up, protesting the government's land acquisition policies and the compensation offered. The Trinamool Congress staged blockades, protests and strikes, and after 14 villagers were killed in police firing, the Left Front government shelved the proposed chemical hub project. Mamata gained politically from Nandigram and Trinamool's performance improved in the Panchayat election in 2008, in which they won two Zilla Parishad polls.

In 2008, Mamata drew international media attention by stopping Tata Motors's dream project to build the world's cheapest car, the Nano, in Singur. This project was again mired in controversy over the way land was acquired for it, the government having invoked a legislation from 1894 meant for land acquisition for public purposes in order to acquire land for a private entity. The land that had been acquired was also some of the most fertile in Bengal, and most families in that region depended on agriculture for their livelihood. The compensation to the villagers about to be displaced was deemed unsatisfactory, and those who had been affected launched protests. Mamata Banerjee went on an indefinite *dharna* outside the Block Development Officer's office in Singur, and called for a road and rail blockade in the area. The national highway running along Singur was blockaded, and Mamata boycotted all-party talks attempting to broker peace. Finally, in 2008, the Tatas moved the project from Singur to Gujarat.

Mamata answered the Left Front's accusations of having been helping Maoists by winning 19 parliamentary seats from Bengal in the 2009 election. In June 2010, the Trinamool Congress fought municipal election alone, without the support of the Congress, and registered a landslide victory in 81 civic bodies across the state, including in Kolkata. Mamata has served as India's union minister for railways twice, first in 2002 and then in 2009, and was the first woman to that office.

Finally, in 2011, Mamata led her party to a spectacular victory, winning 184 of the 294 seats in the assembly, a stupendous gain of 154 seats. The CPI (M), the major party in the Left Front, was utterly humiliated, losing 136 seats and being reduced to only 40 seats in the assembly, with incumbent Chief Minister Buddhadeb Bhattacharya losing from his long-time constituency, Jadavpur. From 30 seats in the previous assembly election in 2006 to 184, Mamata had completely upturned the political landscape of Bengal. Addressing a huge gathering of supporters outside her Kalighat residence, Mamata Banerjee termed her win a victory of democracy, of '*ma-mati-manush*' (mother, land and people).

Biographer Monobina Gupta, in her book *Didi: A Political Biography*, pointed at Mamata's trademark simplicity as one reason for her immense popularity among the masses. The white sari with a thin coloured border, the hair pulled back into a bun and the rubber slippers helped Mamata manipulate an environment dominated by the media. Where Buddhadeb Bhattacharya used a jeep on his political rallies, Mamata walked, sweating, for kilometres meeting people and shaking hands, realizing perfectly well the 'blood, sweat and tears' impression that it would create. When she became chief minister, Mamata declined to move to the chief ministerial bungalow, and preferred to move about in a small private car instead of an official vehicle. Author Sagarika Ghosh has described Mamata as 'India's Lech Walesa' and has remarked that while Mamata was a home-grown anti-communist hero, ironically her self-image was that of a Leftist. Bigness seemed to offend Mamata's lively sense of aesthetics, Ghosh observed.

Monobina Gupta maintains that Mamata does not fit the frame of the stereotypical respect-worthy 'good, maternal, married' Bengali woman, which the CPM admires. According to Gupta, Mamata's lower-middle-class origins, her abrasive, forthright style and jarring and unpolished language remove her from the realm of the genteel '*bhadramahila*'. Till the Singur and Nandigram movements exploded in the CPM's face, Bengal's middle and upper middle classes too were distinctly uncomfortable with Banerjee's lack of grace, her dressing sense, and her subaltern style and syntax of communication.

While Mamata claimed that she would lead a more inclusive government, and abjure the 'communist politics of control', the Trinamool Congress's first term in government was marked by incidents of cadre-based violence, attempts to take control of various arms of the state and political intimidation. The Sharada Group financial scandal, exposés that showed Trinamool ministers accepting bribes, and the collapse of a flyover in one of the busiest parts of the city were other incidents that erupted during her first term. There was also an outbreak of rioting in Kaliachak in Malda, which the BJP, looking to gain a foothold in the state, termed as communal violence targeting Hindus.

Mamata, however, returned to power in 2016 with an increased majority, winning 211 of 294 seats despite the Congress and the Left forming an alliance, and the BJP trying to occupy the Opposition's space. There were many factors that helped Mamata retain power. The Left front's alliance with the Congress, contradictorily, drove many voters to Mamata. The alliance was formed late and lacked popular support among both the Left and the Congress cadres.

On the other hand, Mamata expanded her support base among students. Her position was strengthened by the popular programmes she launched, such as the 'Kanyashree' scheme that offered a monthly scholarship of ₹750 to girls from financially weak families and the 'Sabuj Sathi' scheme that provided cycles to students across towns and villages. Mamata also doled out ₹1,500 each per month to one lakh unemployed youth in the state under the 'Yuvashree' scheme, calling it an 'assistance' to meet their expenses. Similarly, food security for the poor turned out to be big draw in the state. Under the 'Khadya Sathi' scheme, her government offered rice and wheat at ₹2 per kg to around seven crore people. These seven crore people included people living in the Maoist-troubled Jangalmahal region; drought-affected people of Purulia district; malnourished tea garden workers and their families; those affected by recent cyclones; people of Singur who had lost their land due to land acquisition; and other homeless people in the state. Such populist schemes have helped her tremendously in expanding her reach.

While Mamata's chief ministerial terms have been marred by incidents of communal violence, which the BJP has attempted to capitalize on, and political violence, seen as a disappointing continuation of the political violence that has plagued the state for a long time, she has strongly positioned herself as the chief opposition to the BJP and forces propagating Hindutva in the country. She has extended offers of protection to actors and writers who have run afoul of religious extremists, and has often spoken out against communal violence in other parts of the country.

Interestingly, much like the Left Front campaigned to change how central government funds were distributed to state governments, Mamata too has protested vigorously against the central government's one-time demonetization of high-denomination currency in 2016, and the imposition of the Goods and Services Tax (GST) in 2017. Indeed, she is now, according to her opponents, following in the footsteps of the Left Front, whom she had opposed and displaced. Whatever be her electoral fortunes in the future, her grit and determination, firebrand image and distinct mode of leadership have firmly established her as someone who cannot be ignored.

AFTERWORD

Mohan Lal Dhartipakad, a cloth merchant by profession, lost every election he had fought in his eventful political career spread over four decades. Kaka Joginder Singh holds a record of contesting over 350 elections, including for the post of the President of India, to the Lok Sabha, the Rajya Sabha, the Vidhan Sabha and the Vidhan Parishad. Chowdhury Hari Ram, a farmer from Haryana, contested the presidential polls in 1952, 1957, 1962, 1967 and 1969, sometimes getting zero votes. Independent candidates all, they never took their participation in elections lightly. As Dhartipakad said in an interview, 'The idea of contesting at all levels of democracy was to make everyone realize that democracy was meant for one and all and we should all feel part of it.'

Another famous Independent, Nagarmal Bajoria, a trader and social worker based in Bhagalpur who migrated to Bihar from Lahore after the Partition, has had a life-long obsession with contesting polls. At 87 years of age, in 2014, Bajoria fought against Narendra Modi and Arvind Kejriwal from Varanasi on the strength of his slogan '*Ek Bihari sab par bhaari*'. His nomination papers were rejected on a technical ground, but Bajoria was happy to have made the attempt. A veteran of 278 elections – from presidential elections to the local civic polls – Bajoria has the distinction of contesting elections from most states of the country, including the trouble-torn Jammu and Kashmir. Like others of his ilk, Bajoria believes that corruption is the root cause of all the ills plaguing the democratic setup in the country.

According to one estimate, over 40,000 independent candidates have participated in the 16 general elections held since Independence, though most of them have got less than one-sixth of the valid votes polled and thus lost their deposits. Only 214 of them – less than one per cent – have made it to the Parliament.

The oft-overlooked face of democracy is the good fight that is fought by these independent contestants in all elections. In the hullabaloo surrounding political parties, it seems that individual participants in the democratic process are lost in the background. Yet, the provision made in the Constitution of India that any person, regardless of his or her affiliation to a political party, can contest elections as an independent candidate ensures that political parties remain on their toes. And it should not be forgotten that one of the most famous independent candidates in the first general election held in the country was none other than Dr B.R. Ambedkar, one of the chief architects of the Constitution of India, the chairman of the Drafting Committee.

In the 2009 general election, Meera Sanyal, the India head of ABN Amro Bank, who contested against Congress party's Milind Deora for the Mumbai South Lok Sabha seat, strongly disagreed with a remark made by Dr Manmohan Singh, the prime minister at the time, about independent candidates. They were 'spoilers', he had said, and voters should not vote for them. Expressing her respect for Manmohan Singh as a prime minister and an economist, she emphasized that she was not a destabilizing force and was contesting the election for what she believed in. Reminding everyone that India was a democracy, she reaffirmed every citizen's right to contest elections. Sanyal also noted that Prime Minister Singh's statements were a sign that Independents were getting the attention they deserved.

In recent years, not only have prominent citizens from different walks of life entered the political scenario, but newer movements have also given fresh impetus to the polity. The rise and spectacular success of the Aam Aadmi Party in Delhi and Punjab stands testimony to a sense of disillusionment among citizens with organized, traditional political parties. The AAP grew vertically on the planks of accountability and transparency, breaking the horizontal blocs of caste and religion. In 2017, a trio of young leaders – Jignesh Mevani, Alpesh Thakor and Hardik Patel – gave the incumbent BJP a tough fight in Narendra Modi's home state of Gujarat. Jignesh, a vocal supporter of Dalit rights, emerged into prominence when he protested the flogging of Dalit youths for skinning dead cows in Una, Gujarat. Mevani mobilized over 20,000 Dalits, who pledged to give up removing cow carcasses and cleaning gutters, in August 2016. In December 2017, with the support of the Congress, Mevani contested the state elections from the Vadgam constituency as an independent candidate and won by a large margin, stunning the BJP. In Tamil Nadu, two leading actors, Rajinikanth and Kamal Haasan, announced at the end of 2017 that they would be floating regional parties to take on the AIADMK and DMK, who have been holding power in the state since the 1960s. Both Rajinikanth and Kamal Haasan offered an agenda and programmes that were drastically different from those of the organized parties.

In fact, the extent of this dissatisfaction with the existing political order can also be seen in the rising trend of votes won by the NOTA (or none of the above) button in elections since it was first introduced in the 2014 general election. In the 2017 assembly election in Gujarat, 1.8 per cent of all voters chose to reject all candidates. In the Tamil Nadu assembly election held in 2016, the number of votes for NOTA exceeded the victory margin in 25 of the 232 seats. While a NOTA result from an electoral seat does not result in re-election, and hence its relevance is frequently debated, it does very explicitly state the people's mandate.

These experiments in the political playing field prove the vibrancy of democracy in India and indicate that the faith reposed in 'the practical common sense of the common man' has not been in vain after all.

BIBLIOGRAPHY

'India: Cymbals and symbols', *Time*, 28 January 1952.

'PM wants Rahul Gandhi to join Union Cabinet', *News 18*, 21 December 2009.

'The campaign: A winning strategy', *India Today*, 22 November 2013.

Adams, Jad and Philips Whitehead, *The Dynasty: The Nehru–Gandhi Story*, New Delhi: Penguin Books India, 1997.

Aiyar, V. Shankar, 'Tiger in trouble', *India Today*, 17 August 1998.

Anandan, Sujata, *Hindu Hriday Samrat: How the Shiv Sena Changed Mumbai Forever*, New Delhi: HarperCollins Publishers India, 2014.

Ananth, Krishna V., 'Why 1967 general election was a watershed in Indian politics and the lessons it left behind', *DNA,* 22 February 2017.

Bharti, Kanval, '*Baspa aur Dalit Andhanukaran*', New Delhi: *Dalit Liberation Today*, 2 (4) August 1996.

Biswas, Avijit, 'Dhartipakad's next targets Modi, Kejriwal', *Hindustan Times,* 20 March 2014.

Darapuri, S.R., 'Why Dalits have slammed Mayawati's sarvjan rule', Countercurrents.org, 25 March 2012.

Deshmukh, Nanaji, 'RSS and the 1984 pogrom', *People's Democracy,* 21 August 2005.

Deshmukh, Nanaji, 'Moments of soul searching', *Pratipaksh.*

Falk, Bertil, *Feroze: The Forgotten Gandhi,* New Delhi: Roli Books, 2016.

'Labour in Indian agriculture – A growing challenge', FICCI-KPMG, http://ficci.in/spdocument/20550/FICCI-agri-Report%2009-03-2015.pdf.

Frank, Katherine, *Indira: The Life of Indira Nehru Gandhi,* London: Houghton Mifflin, 2002.

Ghoshal, Jayanta, *Didi: The Bengal Tigress,* New Delhi: Juggernaut Books, 2016.

Gill, S.S, *The Dynasty: A Political Biography of the Premier Ruling Family of Modern India,* New Delhi: HarperCollins Publishers India, 1996.

Gupta, Monobina, *Didi: A Political Biography,* New Delhi: HarperCollins Publishers India, 2012.

Gupta, Shekhar, 'National interest: UPA3, the chance', *Indian Express*, 23 June 2012.

Hutheesing, Krishna Nehru, *Dear To Behold: An Intimate Portrait of Indira Gandhi*, London: Macmillan Company, 1969.

Jayakar, Pupul, *Indira Gandhi*, New Delhi: Penguin Books India, 1992.

Johari, J.C., *Indian National Congress since Independence,* New Delhi: Lotus Press, 2006.

Ketkar, Kumar, 'Bal Thackeray: A legacy of pride and identity', *DNA*, 18 November 2012.

Kidwai, Rasheed, 24, *Akbar Road: A Short History of the People behind the Fall and Rise of the Congress*, New Delhi: Hachette India, 2011.

Kidwai, Rasheed, *Sonia: A Biography*, New Delhi: Penguin Books India, 2003.

Kumar, Dilip, *The Substance and the Shadow: An Autobiography as Narrated to Udayatara Nayar,* New Delhi: Hay House, 2014.

Kumar, Vivek and Sinha Uday, 'Dalit assertion and the Bahujan Samaj Party', Bahujan Sahitya Sansthan, 2001.

Mani, Prem Kumar, '*Kiski puja kar rahe hain bahujan*', *Forward Press,* 1 February 2014.

Mitra, Sumit, 'Authority above power', The *Telegraph*, 19 May 2004.

Mukherjee, Pranab, *The Coalition Years 1996–2012,* New Delhi: Rupa Publications, 2017.

Mukherjee, Pranab, *The Dramatic Decade: The Indira Years,* New Delhi: Rupa Publications, 2014.

Mukherjee, Pranab, *The Turbulent Years 1980–1996,* New Delhi: Rupa Publications, 2016.

Narayan, Badri, *Women Heroes and Dalit Assertion in North India: Culture, Identity and Politics,* New Delhi: Sage Publication, 2006.

Pathare, Vrunda, Godrej Archives, Oral History Collection, http://archives.godrej.com.

Rajagopal, Arvind, *Politics after Television: Hindu Nationalism and Reshaping of Public in India,* New Delhi: Cambridge University Press, 2001.

Ramaseshan, Radhika: 'Rajiv shadow in Rahul snub', *Telegraph*, 30 March 2008.

Rao, Daggubati Venkateswara, edited and narrated in English by M. Rafi, *The Other Side of the Truth*, Hyderabad: Nivedita Publication, 2009.

Rao, Keshav Dasu, 'The mother of all rath yatras', *The Hindu*, 1 April 2004.

Sahgal, Priya, 'Bollywood MPs', *India Today*, March 2005.

Sanghvi, Vir, 'The only language Thackeray understands is strength', www.virsanghvi.com, 6 February 2010.

Sen, Sukumar, *Report of the First General Election in India 1951–52 Volume One*, New Delhi: Election Commission of India, 1952.

Tunzelmann, Alex Von, *Indian Summer: The Secret History of the End of an Empire*, United Kingdom: Pocket Books, 2007.

Uzair, Sheikh Mohammad, 'BSP's rout in UP election could likely be the end of Kanshi Ram and Mayawati's movement for social justice: Dalit voices', *India.com*, 13 March 2010.

ACKNOWLEDGEMENTS

I owe this book to my friend and publisher Poulomi Chatterjee, who brought me the idea while we were giving final touches to another book.

Special thanks to the editor-in-chief of the *Telegraph*, Mr Arup Sarkar, and Manini Chatterjee, R. Rajagopal and Sankarshan Thakur, for their constant help and support.

Sincere thanks to Rama Lakshmi, Rajnish Ahuja, Nirmal Pathak, Priya Sahgal, Anita Katyal, Sunetra Choudhury, Sudeep Mukhia, Sheela Bhatt, Radhika Ramaseshan, Richa Sharma, Swaraj Thapa and Farhan Ansari for their precious suggestions and critical comments.

A big thank you to the staff of the magnificent library at the India International Centre (IIC). The library was extremely useful for research and reference material.

To Neelakantan K.K. and Arushi Pareek, who helped in editing and polishing up the manuscript.

And, always, my wife Dr Farah Kidwai for her unfailing support and wit. Falah, Abaan, Inaya, Shad, Safia, Ibrahim, Sami and Samarah for being a source of joy and pride.

ALSO BY THE SAME AUTHOR

24 AKBAR ROAD

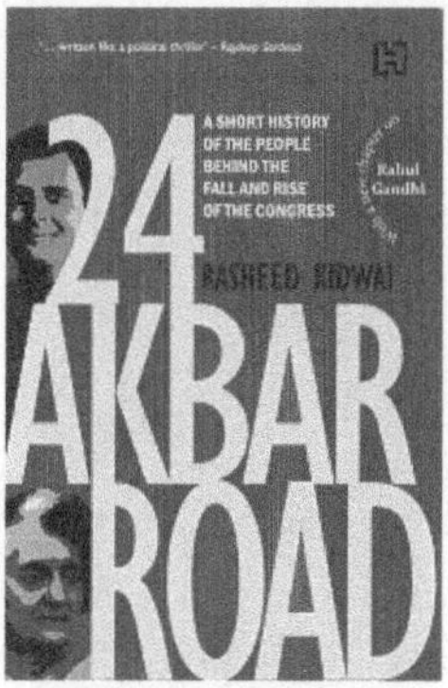

Rs 399

'An absorbing tale rather than a scholarly history, written in a racy style... [A]n enjoyable read.' – *Outlook*

'Here is the stuff of fiction, found in real men and women who matter – from manipulation and intrigue to assertions of power, from the humdrum details of life to the pinnacles of tragedy.' – *Telegraph*

'It is a book that will be a talking point in Congress circles – and beyond – for a long time to come.' – *Hindustan Times*

In his bestselling book, *24 Akbar Road,* seasoned journalist and veteran Congress-watcher Rasheed Kidwai puts together an incisive and engaging account of the Congress's shape-shifting nature and its tenuous hold at the Centre, providing a dispassionate observer's glance at affairs within the party. Kidwai brilliantly tracks the story of the contemporary Congress in the years after the Emergency, using the party's seat of power at 24 Akbar Road as his vantage to draw a compelling account of its leadership from Indira, Sanjay and Rajiv Gandhi to Narasimha Rao and Sitaram Kesri, to the trinity of Sonia Gandhi, Manmohan Singh and Rahul Gandhi.

ALSO BY THE SAME AUTHOR

NETA ABHINETA: BOLLYWOOD STAR POWER IN INDIAN POLITICS

Rs 599

'Abundant in precious anecdotes about iconic films and political personalities.' – *Deccan Herald*

'The rare anecdotes and popular gossip make it an excellent book. Those weaned on Bollywood, its actors and their capers, will find this book worth lapping [up].' – *Free Press Journal*

What draws the larger-than-life personalities who entertain us on-screen to the world of governance and politics off-screen?

Neta Abhineta: Bollywood Star Power in Indian Politics traces this phenomenon through intimate and compelling portrayals of some of the most popular actors in Hindi cinema who have, from the years leading up to India's independence in 1947, entered Indian politics for reasons ranging from a sense of social commitment to a desperate quest for a second chance at fame when their star power dimmed. Dilip Kumar, Nargis and Sunil Dutt, Rajesh Khanna, Jaya and Amitabh Bachchan, Shatrughan Sinha, Hema Malini, Mithun Chakraborty, Jaya Prada, Vinod Khanna, Govinda, Raj Babbar and Paresh Rawal are some of the more prominent names that feature in this engaging account involving film veterans, superstars and also-rans.

Blending history with hard facts and entertaining anecdotes about personal and professional rivalries, clandestine romantic liaisons and cruel betrayals, Rasheed Kidwai presents a potent cocktail. With its clear-eyed perspective on the peculiar nature of Indian politics, this book reveals what ensues when the two worlds – as intensely alluring as they are dangerously fickle – merge.